STUDIES IN ENGLISH LITERATURES

Edited by Koray Melikoğlu

Melanie Ann Hanson

Decapitation and Disgorgement

The Female Body's Text
in Early Modern English Drama and Poetry

D1722158

STUDIES IN ENGLISH LITERATURES

Edited by Koray Melikoğlu

ISSN 1614-4651

1   *Özden Sözalan*
The Staged Encounter
Contemporary Feminism and Women's Drama
2nd, revised editon
ISBN 3-89821-367-6

2   *Paul Fox (ed.)*
Decadences
Morality and Aesthetics in British Literature
ISBN 3-89821-573-3

3   *Daniel M. Shea*
James Joyce and the Mythology of Modernism
ISBN 3-89821-574-1

4   *Paul Fox and Koray Melikoğlu (eds.)*
Formal Investigations
Aesthetic Style in Late-Victorian and Edwardian Detective Fiction
ISBN 978-3-89821-593-0

5   *David Ellis*
Writing Home
Black Writing in Britain Since the War
ISBN 978-3-89821-591-6

6   *Wei H. Kao*
The Formation of an Irish Literary Canon in the Mid-Twentieth Century
ISBN 978-3-89821-545-9

7   *Bianca Del Villano*
Ghostly Alterities
Spectrality and Contemporary Literatures in English
ISBN 978-3-89821-714-9

8   *Melanie Ann Hanson*
Decapitation and Disgorgement
The Female Body's Text in Early Modern English Drama and Poetry
ISBN 978-3-89821-605-5

9   *Shafquat Towheed (ed.)*
New Readings in the Literature of British India, c.1780-1947
ISBN 978-3-89821-673-9

Melanie Ann Hanson

DECAPITATION AND DISGORGEMENT

The Female Body's Text
in Early Modern English Drama and Poetry

ibidem-Verlag
Stuttgart

Bibliografische Information der Deutschen Nationalbibliothek
Die Deutsche Nationalbibliothek verzeichnet diese Publikation in der Deutschen Nationalbibliografie; detaillierte bibliografische Daten sind im Internet über http://dnb.d-nb.de abrufbar.

Bibliographic information published by the Deutsche Nationalbibliothek
Die Deutsche Nationalbibliothek lists this publication in the Deutsche Nationalbibliografie; detailed bibliographic data are available in the Internet at http://dnb.d-nb.de.

Cover illustration:
Pieter Paul Rubens (with Frans Snyders): The Head of Medusa, c. 1617.

∞

Gedruckt auf alterungsbeständigem, säurefreien Papier
Printed on acid-free paper

ISSN: 1614-4651

ISBN-10: 3-89821-605-5
ISBN-13: 978-3-89821-605-0

© *ibidem*-Verlag
Stuttgart 2007

Printed in Germany

For my parents,
Milford and Florine Hanson

Your abiding love, support, and encouragement
made this book, and many things in my life, possible

Contents

Acknowledgments

There are many individuals who helped this study come into being. I wish to express my appreciation to Evelyn Gajowski who was instrumental in the development of this book. In addition, I am grateful to Charles Whitney, John Irsfeld, and Joseph McCullough, who encouraged my research in Early Modern English literature and my professional pursuits.

INTRODUCTION

This study continues the work of post-modernist French feminists who interrogate the empowering and disempowering constructs of language, its subtext and meanings, the *entredeux*, or in-between, area between words in binary opposition, and texts that can only be revealed by the female body. The four chapters of this study attempt to explore the portrayal of female characters in Early Modern English drama and poetry; they analyze the work of women writers with the aim of reworking the literary canon, reveal the silencing effects of patriarchal ideology, contribute to a discussion of women's culture and *herstory*, and value women's experiences, thereby emulating aspects of the American feminist project. This work also dialogues with psychoanalytic feminist discourse that concentrates on examining phallogocentric societies and thinking, discovers competing desires of characters, and explores the similarities and differences between female and male characters and female and male authors, in this case, from Early Modern England.

Certain works were paramount to the shaping of this study. Gerda Lerner's article "Veiling the Woman" and Howard Eilberg-Schwartz and Wendy Doniger's *Off With her Head* helped me to pinpoint my definition of figurative decapitation, a consuming of the female head into the female body as just another sexual part. Sandra Bartky's interpretation of Michel Foucault's panopticism, the concept that women have an internal eye of surveillance because they are treated as sexual objects, gave birth to sections of my book on the debilitating aspects of beauty, especially concerning Mariam's relationship to Herod and Whitney's description of London as a fickle suitor who trivializes the narrator in "The Manner of Her Will." Sections of this book also build upon the critical works of Janet Adelman and the relation of men and women to phallogocentric societies and the import of the mother, and of Trinh Minh-ha and the assertion that women write their whole body and that women's writing resists the body's separation. Pamela Banting's article spoke to me, especially her clear re-interpretation and updating of Hélène Cixous's theories. My book reflects my interest in Susan Gubar's discussion of the power of the pen(is) over woman as blank page and Evelyn Gajowski's application of the blank page to Lavinia. Certain parts of this study, the section of the chapters on "*jouissance* through bisexual discourse" in particular, are influenced by David Willburn's theories concerning somethingness in nothingness. Julie Taymor's film version of *Titus Andronicus* and Lisa Starks's essay on the film that applies Julia Kristeva's idea of the *abject* to Taymor's film adaptation assisted me in my exploration of monstrous and nurturing mothers in chapters 1 and 2.

In particular, the observations of French feminist Hélène Cixous, especially her work from the twentieth century, are instructive when interrogating Early Modern English texts. Cixous applied her theories to a variety of fiction and non-fiction pieces from disparate time periods and societies including the works of Aeschylus, William Shakespeare, Fyodor Dostoevsky, Franz Kafka, Edgar Allan Poe, Søren Kierkegaard, and Sun Tse. In this book, Cixous's ideas are applied to Early Modern texts of Elizabeth Cary, William Shakespeare, John Milton, and Isabella Whitney. Cixous's ideas and semantics are used here as tools for the discernment of women's voices, fictive or real, that have been stifled by those in power and yet despite this obstruction, or maybe because of it, are still recognizable if writers and readers are willing to investigate them. The female body struggling to express text is what first intrigued me about the study of English Renaissance literature.

The idea of the female body, truncated by the oppressive elements in society but continuing to outpour text, is what led me to the writing of Hélène Cixous. In an odd way, wanting to understand Early Modern English drama and poetry, authored by women in particular, lead me to Cixous, and then reading Cixous led me back to the great richness of female expression in Renaissance England. Cary and Whitney, female writers of this period in England, were, like Cixous, interested in how to express a text despite the restrictions put on women's speech and writing. Notwithstanding the fact that Early Modern Englishwomen's lives were dictated, for the most part, by a society governed by men, there were women born into different classes who tried to convey their situation to others.

They attempted to tell their stories through their writing. They often used the types of writing that were considered appropriate for women to create (private correspondence, poetic translation, the closet drama) as the vehicles for their texts. These female authors undermined the purpose of the kinds of linguistic practices and language constructs that were popular with male writers in their time period; the Petrarchan blazon[1] and Ovidian[2] discourse, apparent in pamphlets and conduct manuals, were used to train men to control and mold female behavior. Women writers reversed the expectations in the literary community concerning these constructs to assist in voicing their desires. Women like Anne Askew, Mary Sidney, Mary Wroth, Amelia Lanyer, and Aphra Behn wanted their voices to go on record concerning the condition of women's lives in sixteenth- and seventeenth-century England.

In addition to these women, male writers like Shakespeare exposed the brutality of female oppression through their work. Shakespeare was

---

[1] A poetic convention designed to idealize women. The blazon was popularly used in sonnets written in Italy and England during the Renaissance but actually dates back to ancient Sumerian poetry. The convention uses a string of metaphors to compare female body parts to objects in nature, like fruit or the stars, to pay tribute to female beauty. The female body is thus anatomized in poetic form.

[2] A term used to describe writing that denigrates women. Contemporary U.S. feminist academics use the term 'Ovidian discourse' when referring in their research to texts that describe women in an insulting or ridiculing manner. The term 'Ovidian' is due to the patronizing tone towards women in works like Ovid's *Ars Amatoria*.

not alone in his exploration of the female body's text; men like Edmund Spenser, Philip Sidney, John Ford, and John Webster facilitated the release of women's voices through the female characters and narrators depicted in their poetry and drama. Spenser's Britomart in *The Fairie Queene*, Sidney's Philoclea in *The Countess of Pembroke's Arcadia*, Ford's Penthea in *The Broken Heart*, and Webster's title character in *The Duchess of Malfi* add their perspectives to the dialogue concerning the manipulation of female voice and sexuality.

Privileging the female body's text and discussing the variety of means used to speak it is a central concern of this study. The body can express text in a variety of ways including writing, speaking, gesturing, and so on. Michel de Montaigne, a contemporary of Shakespeare's, was cognizant of the body's propensity to express text:

> What doe we with our hands? Doe we not sue and entreate, promise and performe, call men unto us, and discharge them, bid them farewell, and be gone, threaten, pray, beseech, deny, refuse, demaund, admire, number, confesse, repent, [. . .] declare silence and astonishment? And what not? With so great variation, and amplifying, as if they would contend with the tongue. And with our head, doe we not envite and call to-us, discharge and send away, avowe, disavowe, be-lie, welcome, honour, worship, disdaine, demaund [. . .]? What do-we with our eye-lids? And with our shoulders? To conclude, there is no motion, nor jesture, that doth not speake, and speakes in language [. . .] common and publicke to all: whereby it followeth (seeing the varieties, and severall use it hath from others) that this must rather be deemed the proper and peculier speech of humane nature. (17)

Montaigne's lengthy, descriptive litany, although intending to privilege the body's text, reveals that words are often privileged over the text of the body. Also, the male body's text in the past has been privileged over the female body's text. It is the function of this text, however, to discuss and spotlight the latter.

The texts of Early Modern English dramatists and poets use subversive tactics, including merging with accepted authorial practices, to express feelings and to outpour commentary about what the female body's experience was like during this era. A merging with acceptable male texts, a bisexual discourse, is not suppression and is not submission. Instead, bisexual discourse is a means to display generosity, which is the point of writing. Writing is a giving, not a taking. Women writers in Early Modern England did not submit; they manipulated their positions in society, the roles of the obedient, kind, faithful, chaste, silent female, as a method to create voice.

The project of this book is to illustrate how, using Cixous's psychoanalytic theories, the application of notions like decapitation, disgorgement, *jouissance*, and *entredeux* can bring the lives of Early Modern English women and their writings into a fresh perspective for a contemporary audience. What is of import here is the connection between silencing and expression that brings about a subversion of discourse through generosity rather than hostility. My project emphasizes bisexual discourse as a means to develop a unique female expression rather than the use of rancor or subterfuge to create a rebellious stance. The expression of text through the development of voice in the characters of Mariam, Lavinia, Eve, and Whitney's narrator is ultimately subversive and not marginalized. Ironically, this is engineered by blending their text with what is stereotypically called male discourse.

I wish to ponder the question that Elaine Showalter and Annette Kolodny have raised: if women become writers and speakers and use language to express their texts, are these texts that are dominated by male control of language then diminished, creating a divided consciousness? I feel that using language as a translating medium enhances the female body's text. I agree with Pamela Banting's assessment of Cixous's theory that women use patriarchal discourse as a source language to translate the female body's text, a source language that women dislocate, explode, contain, and translate (235). My research dialogues with other feminist writers who are interested in ways the female body *speaks* its text.

In this book, I examine how Lavinia's repeated presence on stage reveals her character as absent signifier in *Titus Andronicus*, and I apply this idea to how Herod's wives are characterized as absent signifiers in *The Tragedy of Mariam*, how Milton reveals Eve to be an absent signifier in *Paradise Lost*, and how women of the gentry like Whitney were treated as absent signifiers by members of the aristocracy. These four female characters use the body to express their text despite all obstacles.

It would be difficult, if not impossible, to read this book without an orientation to the theoretical framework and terminology that inspired it. Cixous defines decapitation as a figurative beheading by which a patriarchal society manipulates and controls a woman's voice and her sexuality ("Castration" 163). Since men feel figuratively castrated by what they define as female chaos, according to Sigmund Freud, they feel they must restore and maintain order via the figurative decapitation of women. I view decapitation as an envisioning of the woman as blank page, an entity to be composed by men, applying here the work of Susan Gubar (295). Men in a patriarchy re-inscribe the female body with their own meanings, thus decapitating the woman and rewriting her text. I concur with Howard Eilberg-Schwartz and Wendy Doniger, who argue that eroticizing the female head identifies it as another part of the sexualized female body, the female as all flesh (1). Therefore, the female face, eyes, voice, mouth, hair are all part of the erotic experience. The head becomes submerged; it disappears into the body. Veiling the head is just another form of figurative decapitation in the respect that the head disappears, and as it vanishes, it is further eroticized as a symbol of desire submerged into the body (Eilberg-Schwartz and Doniger 2). Makeup and corrective surgery hide and eroticize the real face and are yet other forms of figurative decapitation. I also agree with Eilberg-Schwartz and Doniger that figurative decapitation insures that the female body is blind, voiceless, and invisible (15).

Men cut away aspects of femininity they feel they cannot control, replacing these with constructs of what it is to be female according to men. A body that is segmented is not whole. I see figurative decapitation as a segmenting of each woman's body as well as of the female communal body. A female cut away from the feminine community has no support group or role models; she is isolated and alone. Women in past centuries were expected to stay at home to cook, clean, and tend children. These women were often alienated from their peer group. The figuratively decapitated woman is organized and compartmentalized by the patriarchy; she is told who she is and how she should behave because she is headless. Women should be wives, mothers, sisters, daughters, mistresses, housekeepers, seamstresses, but they should not be subjects. Not only are the roles of the decapitated female defined, but her sexuality is controlled by the patriarchy as well. Therefore, women are beheaded in more than one way. The beheading of women's sexuality puts all forms of female birthing and creativity under the control of men. Women in past eras were passed from father to husband as property in arranged marriage. Therefore, decapitation can be viewed as figurative rape, a violation of the female body and its text. If a woman does not surrender to the patriarchal conditioning, she will experience psychological and physical violence to bring her under control. However, this does not mean that women in abusive cultures are completely powerless. Those in authority just think they are.

Women have no access to language and law, because language and law are part of the masculine domain. Therefore, to communicate, women in repressive cultures find means to use their figurative decapitation to their own advantage. Language is used to control women. Petrarchan and Ovidian discourse re-inscribe the female body. Petrarchan discourse refers to language that idealizes women as do the sonnets of Francesco Petrarch. Petrarchan poetic conventions were adapted by English writers during the English Renaissance. Petrarchan discourse figuratively decapitates women by turning real women into the idealistic creation of the male imagination. Ovidian discourse is being used in a specific context in this project that differs slightly from ordinary scholarly usage. I use the term 'Ovidian' to allude to Ovid's treatment of women, particularly in *Ars amatoria,* where the author gives young men in his society advice on how to woo and entrap women, constructing women as mere sex objects. Because of its more explicit concern with seduction, Ovidian discourse also figuratively decapitates.

The archetype of the beheaded female is Medusa from mythology. Men see her as monstrous, but Cixous reworks the Medusa figure. In the essay "The Laugh of the Medusa," Cixous characterizes femaleness independent of male mythologies. Cixous' Medusa "breaks the codes that negate her" (879). "[Medusa is] beautiful and she's laughing" (885). In this way, Cixous characterizes an *entredeux* discourse for women. The male myth of Medusa as monstrous is deconstructed by *l'écriture féminine*.

All women are like the beheaded Medusa. Men have defined the parameters of what it is to be female; the stereotype is nurturing and accepting. Cixous embraces this marginalized position as well, because women can use the stereotype (woman as body in juxtaposition to man as head) to their advantage. Since "women are body" ("Laugh" 886), they can use the body as text. A woman who creates *l'écriture féminine* by using the body as text is "ceasing to support with her body [. . .] the general cultural heterosocial establishment in which man's reign is held to be proper [. . .] the 'proper' is property" ("Castration" 171). A woman's body is disorder, passions, creativity – this is her text. Medusa's laughter disrupts. The male myth of Medusa as monstrous is deconstructed by *l'écriture feminine*.

Introduction

Medusa has much in common with the female characters discussed in this book. Lavinia, like Medusa, is a maid at the opening of Shakespeare's *Titus Andronicus* who is transformed, through her encounter with the characters Demetrius and Chiron, into a monster. Lavinia and Medusa are not only physically monstrous; they also represent patriarchal fear of repressed secret emotions and repressed rage and pain. In Ovid's version of the story of Medusa, the beauty of Medusa's hair and body as a maiden are described, but her face is not delineated. Therefore, Ovid figuratively beheads and objectifies Medusa. Lavinia, like Medusa, is the object of the male gaze, but we see very little of her interior self. Lavinia and Medusa are speechless throughout most of the text and we do not hear their reaction to their physical transformation (Walker 50). Both have jealous suitors who rival for their attention. They are victimized by their rapists, and Tamora, like Athena, turns a blind eye to the rape. Tamora and Athena enable the oppression of their rivals.

Poseidon transformed himself into a stallion and the beautiful Medusa into a mare so that he might ravage her. In Julie Taymor's film version of *Titus Andronicus*, Lavinia appears transformed, like Medusa in the legend, with the head of a doe as Tamora's sons rape her in the guise of raging tigers (Starks 8). Medusa was the daughter of Phorcys, a lesser god who as the son of earth and sea was linked to Poseidon, Medusa's rapist. Medusa's beauty is blamed for the rape (Valentis and Devane 43). Demetrius and Chiron are enticed by Lavinia's beauty and innocence as well. Raping Lavinia will make her ugly; it will turn Lavinia into the monstrous mother. Medusa's gaze turned men to stone; in other words, men were sexually excited and at the same time terrified of Medusa.

Demetrius and Chiron see Lavinia and Tamora, their mother, in this same regard. In Lavinia's case, Demetrius and Chiron are sexually aroused by her but know that possessing her will be risky. The risk is also part of the attraction. They rape Lavinia as a substitute for the mother they want to possess and conquer. Perseus and Tamora's sons kill the sexual potency and matriarchal rule of the mother through a beheading, literal in Medusa's case (standing in for Perseus' mother, Danae) and figurative in Lavinia's. The relationship of motherhood to decapitation and disgorgement is examined in this book not only through the character of Lavinia but also through Mariam, Eve, and Whitney's poetic narrative voices. Medusa is Cixous's icon for the merging of decapitation with disgorgement.

A way to use figurative decapitation to create text is through what Cixous calls disgorgement, a vomiting of indigestible patriarchal constructs. Disgorgement "splits open the closure of binary oppositions," as Toril Moi puts it (106). In Cixous's theories, decapitation facilitates disgorgement because the decapitated female becomes an entity with no head, no face, no voice, no reason, and therefore one that is unlike the male, revealing rather than concealing, open and vulnerable rather than withholding ("Castration" 176). Decapitation does not accomplish the patriarchal aim of silencing women, because it is a step towards female disgorgement. Cixous sees disgorgement as an outpouring of *l'écriture féminine* or feminine writing as it embraces an *entredeux* position, a bisexual discourse ("Laugh" 884). Bisexual discourse is *entredeux*, because it deconstructs the binary system of male languages. Cixous's use of the term "bisexual" is not necessarily an attempt to discuss the contemporary notion of a person's sexual relations with both women and men; Cixous is using the term to discuss women's discourse or *l'écriture féminine* as a discourse that automatically embraces the female body's text as well as male written and verbal languages. This merger of discourses conjures away the fear of castration, according to Cixous ("Laugh" 884). "Woman is bisexual" to her, because it is part of a woman writer's existence to *speak* by translating the discourse of the female body into the discourse of phallologocentrism.

The term 'phallogocentrism' denotes the view of the phallus and the logos (word, reason) as the creative center of language; phallologocentrism affects power structures, societal mores, and language as well as what and who is defined as proper and as property. Men are born into a phallocentric social order and therefore trained to *speak* from what Cixous names a monosexual position.

Therefore, Cixous rejects the masculine insistence on form, order, wholeness, unity, hierarchy, duality, and linear thinking. Whereas language that labels women as either virgin or whore is decapitating, disgorgement is a discourse that undermines the binary system of language. The binary system of language is a process of labeling in which all things are ordered or positioned in one of two categories; for example, a woman would be characterized as either silent or outspoken, innocent or unchaste, obedient or disruptive, and so on. Cixous believes that male authors and male characters can disgorge, but this happenstance is rare in Early Modern England since men of that time were raised in a patriarchal culture and therefore were trained to embrace dichotomy in discourse. I like to think of disgorgement of the female body's text in the way that Banting does, as corporeal grammatology (231). Banting, interpreting the theories of Cixous, suggests that the female body exudes a kind of language separate from the spoken word, different from the grammar that children learn. Banting's idea of corporeal grammatology is a way of examining Cixous's theory that there is a language between mother and child that gets pushed aside once the child learns to speak and write. The spoken and written word are components of the language of the head, of reason, of the patriarchy. This study attempts to illustrate how Early Modern women were manipulated, identified, and sexualized just as words are by the male-governed society and how these women used their understanding of the verbal decapitation of women as a means to access and express their own corporeal grammatology.

Because the body is susceptible to inscription, it has signifying capabilities. However, the female body's text does not enable nor reinforce patriarchal stereotypes of women; it critiques the male gaze. Cixous's theories of decapitation and disgorgement reverse masculine hierarchy so that the body as text locates lack not within women's sexuality but within mastery and masculinity. Labels put on women's bodies and containment of bodies through the law and through language, as in religious practices and philosophical asceticism, take women away from their bodies and therefore away from using the body's text (Banting 231).

Disgorgement is utter generosity without the hope of return, without the involvement of property or propriety; language, like the male economy, implies an exchange, but disgorgement expects nothing back. Disgorgement is a kind of text that moves beyond the author's intent, and all authors, narrators, and characters disgorge differently. Disgorgement does not remember or reconstruct; rather, it deconstructs ("Laugh" 887). According to Cixous, disgorgement responds to decapitation by utilizing the female body to create an outpouring of the body as text although she envisions an ideal *écriture* that moves beyond masculine or feminine labels.

Cixous defines disgorgement as an outpouring of primeval feminine power or the mother tongue, the site of fragmentation, splitting, and detachment that male society attempts to contain ("Castration" 175). The mother tongue is a special communication, a body language between child and mother that children lose touch with as they are educated into male-governed society and its laws, language, and mores ("Laugh" 234). Cixous sees a woman's body as disorder, passions, creativity – this is her text.

Disgorgement of bodily text escapes the containment of the page and transcends the end of the author's text or the death of a character. Text is often meant to define or contain, but disgorgement is a communication of *jouissance* that does the opposite: it exudes, expresses, and transcends containment (Cixous, "Castration" 170). *Jouissance* is the joy of sensation in all forms. Disgorgement is catalyzed by reveling in figurative *jouissance,* an expression of pleasure derived from the female body's text, an outpouring that has no end and has nothing to do with the male economy of gain, profit, and debt. The term *jouissance* is used figuratively in this text. *Jouissance* is the link between sexuality and textuality; *jouissance* is manifested textually as an overflow of emotion from sexual response. Therefore, *jouissance* is always connected to sexual interplay between women and men or female and male characters. J. C. Smith and Carla Ferstman assert that there are different kinds of *jouissance* and that there can be no *jouissance* without a release of emotion (241). The emotional outpouring in *jouissance* is a part of female disorder that disrupts system and structure. Therefore the outpouring of "emotion becomes an important metaphor for perceived threats to established authority; the emotionality of repressed groups becomes a symbol of their antistructural tendencies. To the powerful, this is their chaos, to the groups themselves, it is their impulse towards freedom" (Lutz 62).

The flow of emotions facilitates disgorgement, the female desire to express. Female expression is a manifestation of generosity, a gift of displaying the female body's desire in various forms. Cixous believes that a woman who disgorges breaks out in endless laughter ("Castration" 177). This laughter can be an expression of joy, of pain, of derision. Through *jouissance*, women can embrace their sexual difference as a disruption of patriarchal discourse, but most often female *jouissance* is a by-product of merging with male forms of expression. Disgorgement is a non-withholding; conversely, figurative decapitation is the containment of *jouissance*. My project is aligned with Cixous's definition of *jouissance*, but I emphasize textual *jouissance* or a merging of discourse that Cixous calls bisexual rather than a discussion of the female characters' sexual responses.

To exact a deeper understanding of decapitation and disgorgement, the influence of Sigmund Freud, Jacques Lacan, and Jacques Derrida on Cixous's work must be addressed. Cixous problematizes Freud's assertion that the phallus is the "primary organizer of the structure of subjectivity" ("Castration" 167) in a patriarchal society. For example, from a Freudian perspective, the male characters' repressed wishes and truncated desires are made manifest in the repression of female *jouissance* in *The Tragedy of Mariam* (chapter 1) and *Titus Andronicus* (chapter 2). It is impossible in patriarchal society to operate outside the phallocentric order, but it is possible to subvert that order from within. Lacan indicates that men are trapped in the system of phallocentrism; he theorizes that as boys grow up they substitute things like language for their relationship to their mother, as Ross Murfin points out (248). French feminists like Cixous *speak* to theories proposed by Lacan and Derrida about male separation anxiety from the mother and how this impacts male separation from the mother tongue.

This project also owes much to Coppelia Kahn, Katherine Rowe, Elaine Beilin, Ann Rosalind Jones, Ana Kothe, Marjorie Garber, Elaine Showalter, Toril Moi, Judith Butler, Lynda Boose, Frances Dolan, Annette Kolodny, Mary Ellen Lamb, Catherine Lutz, Bruce Lincoln, John Berger, and Kate Bornstein; their writing and research stimulated my thoughts on the subject of the female body as text and reading their work inspired me to pursue my ideas about female characters and women writers associated with Early Modern English literature.

In summation, the disgorgement of text can be achieved in a variety of ways: by using language to explore the *entredeux* position between stereotypically male and female discourse, to reveal generosity from the feminine body, or to depict the chaos and fragmentation inscribed on women by patriarchal containment. Cixous indicates that women would disgorge to the death "were it not for the intervention of those basic movements of a feminine unconscious which provide the capacity of passing above it all by means of a form of oblivion which is not the oblivion of burial or interment but the oblivion of acceptance. This is taking loss, seizing it, living it" ("Castration" 176). Cixous's theories have varied applications, and the four chapters of this book will focus on exploring disgorgement in just two specific areas: the subversion of accepted discursive practices and the figurative *jouissance* achieved through creating a merged text or bisexual discourse. Cary's *The Tragedy of Mariam* reveals not only how the body of the title character disorders the male world but also expresses an outpouring of the female body's *jouissance*, as the reader will see in chapter 1.

CHAPTER 1
MARIAM IN ELIZABETH CARY'S
THE TRAGEDY OF MARIAM

Elizabeth Cary uses writing to translate the female body's *jouissance* into language in her closet drama, *The Tragedy of Mariam.* Death, like writing, is a translating medium between the body's text and a statement or expression. Cary and Shakespeare, whose character Lavinia is spotlighted in chapter 2, create female characters whose deaths are a textual disgorgement, an outpouring of feelings and a subversion of language constructs, for the dramatists. The deaths of Lavinia and Mariam are a text of loss, of releasing the voice from containment. Women writers want to translate into language what the body performs naturally. Ironically, giving birth to oneself as a woman sometimes involves a death. A female death is not a glorified martyrdom, a celebration of female death that underscores figurative decapitation by the patriarchy; instead, as Catherine Belsey (190) and Frances Dolan (159) assert, a female presence on the scaffold, like Cary's representation of her character Mariam, expresses text in a way that Early Modern Englishwomen were not permitted at any other time or place. Hélène Cixous believes that women do not give to the point of death, because women embrace "the oblivion of *acceptance*" ("Castration" 176). I agree with this but I also re-envision this oblivion to include death, an argument that this and the following chapter attempt to articulate. Cary's character, Mariam, accepts her fate because she knows that she will go on, residing in heaven in "Sara's lap" (4.8.574).[3] I believe that sometimes women "live loss," as Cixous puts it, through their own deaths.

---

[3] Quotations of Elizabeth Cary's The Tragedy of Mariam are from Margaret W. Ferguson and Barry Weller's The Tragedy of Mariam, the Fair Queen of Jewry with The Lady Falkland; Her Life.

It is my contention that Cary rewrites past history, deconstructs male texts through the veiled discourse of the closet drama and uses this re-telling, this mythmaking in process, to create a disgorgement of text. The author re-creates six female characters (Mariam, Alexandra, Doris, Salome, Graphina, and Cleopatra), sticking closely to the history of Herod the Great laid out in Flavius Josephus's *Antiquities of the Jews* (bk. 14, chs. 12-16 and bk. 15, chs. 1-7). I agree with Alexandra Bennett, who views the female characters in this play as representations of different methods of approaching textuality (298). Cary as a female writer who is rewriting history is actually expressing *herstory*, the saga of women's past experiences as an expression that validates her own life story. Mariam is the key figure in the drama and, like Lavinia in Shakespeare's *Titus Andronicus*, Mariam turns her figurative decapitation into an expression of the female body's text. Cary creates disgorgement through subverting language, disrupting the order of the hierarchy through Mariam's death, and producing *jouissance* through a bisexuality of discourse.

Plot Summary

Herod has ascended the Jewish monarchy with the help of Roman favor and married the rightful king Hyrcanus's daughter, Mariam. To do this, he renounced his wife, Doris, and her children. He then arranged, through various means, for the deaths of Mariam's brother and grandfather to eliminate anyone who might fight him for the throne. He goes to Rome to answer accusations about the murders brought against him by Mariam's mother, Alexandra. The custody of Mariam has been left to Herod's uncle, Josephus, while Herod is away. Josephus is married to Herod's sister, Salome. Herod told Josephus that if anything happened while Herod was in Rome, Josephus was to kill Mariam. He revealed this information to Mariam, and when Herod returned home, she was angry with her husband for more than one reason. Salome manipulates her brother to put Josephus to death so that she can marry Sohemus. Herod is called back once again to Rome due to Caesar's reinstatement to the throne and therefore an alteration in Herod's fortune and position in the government has occurred. News of Herod's death comes to Jerusalem and Mariam hears of it. She is in a quandary as to whether she should be overjoyed or saddened when her husband suddenly appears, and she discovers that the news of his death was simply a rumor. Herod is deeply in love with his wife and tries again and again to get her to forgive him for the deaths of her family members and return his affections. Salome wants to rid the kingdom of Mariam so she plots against her. Salome sends a cup of wine that allegedly contains a love potion that should be given to Herod, but then the delivering servant reveals that the wine really has poison in it. Salome is trying to turn Herod against his wife by making him think that Mariam is trying to kill him. Salome continues to poison Herod's mind against his wife until he decides to put Mariam to death. She goes to her end bearing herself with great nobility and Herod is beside himself with grief and remorse over what he has done.

Figurative Decapitation

> Women have no choice other than to be decapitated [. . .] if they don't actually lose their heads by the sword, *they only keep them on condition that they lose them* – lose them, that is, to complete silence [. . .] If man operates under the threat of castration, if masculinity is culturally ordered by the castration complex, it might be said that the backlash, the return, on women of this castration anxiety is its displacement as decapitation, execution, of woman, as loss of her head. (Cixous, "Castration" 163-64)

Mariam is figuratively and literally decapitated by her husband Herod, catalyzed by his issues concerning masculinity, namely his jealous possessiveness of Mariam. In fact, the female characters are carefully positioned in Cary's play to illustrate different aspects of figurative decapitation, all of which impact Mariam's situation in some manner.

Alexandra, Mariam's mother, blindly enables patriarchal containment, consumption of herself and her daughter, throughout the play, even though she rails against it. In act 1, she objectifies Mariam's beauty when she uses a "portraiture" (2.187) of Mariam's "visage" (2.197) as a snare to catch Marc Antony's attention, but Alexandra's attempts to win favor do not work. Alexandra figuratively decapitates Mariam with her description of the powers of Mariam's beauty over men; Alexandra indicates that in Mariam's visage is an entire assortment of alluring women on display for the highest bidder (1.2.197). Cary characterized her relationship with her own mother as "trying," as Naomi Miller indicates (356); more than once in Cary's biography, *The Lady Falkland; Her Life*, Cary's mother, like Alexandra, enables the figurative decapitation of her daughter.

Alexandra's words in act 1 indicate that women must compete with each other for the favors of men. Doris and Mariam, like Tamora and Lavinia in *Titus Andronicus*, cannot bond because they must vie for male protection and attention; women end up in an adversarial position to maintain their status in relation to men. One example of the separation of women in Mariam's world is at the beginning of act 1 where Mariam reveals that Sohemus saved her from death, that Herod had decreed that she should die if he was killed. Herod intended to figuratively decapitate Mariam even after his demise. Alexandra suggests that Herod may have wanted Mariam dead so that he could return to Doris, Herod's first wife (1.2.128-29). Herod's cruelty is his figurative decapitation of the women in his life (2.3.264). Doris believed Herod's oaths that "affirm'd [her] face without compare" (2.3.240) when they were married. However, this is no longer the case. Doris believes she has lost her position as Herod's queen to Mariam because she was not considered to be "fair enough" compared to Mariam's beauty (2.3.235). Women are judged on their beauty and virtue.

Therefore, in act 2, Doris "begg'd for vengeance" (2.3.247) and for "the fall of her [Mariam] that on my trophy stands" (2.3.250). Doris's statement about the "foul adultery [that] blotteth Mariam's brow" (2.3.278) is conflated with Doris's words about "revenge's foulest spotted face" (2.3.280). Adultery and revenge are depicted as destroying Mariam's beauty and therefore her hold on Herod. Adultery and revenge are joined in language the way Doris and Mariam are connected in the play. However, Doris fears that words will not have the power to heal the wrongs done to her: "Had I ten thousand tongues and ev'ry tongue / Inflam'd with poison's power, and steep'd in gall: / My curses would not answer for my wrong" (4.8.609-11). Doris is completely wrapped up in her son, Antipater, and his position in the hierarchy that has been lost to Mariam's son because Mariam has usurped Doris's position in Herod's court. Doris's words enable the patriarchal control of women, including her own containment. Just as Lavinia kneels to Tamora to beg not for her own life but for Tamora to stop Demetrius and Chiron from violating her in *Titus Andronicus*, Mariam kneels to Doris later in the play to beg not for her own life but for the lives of her children (4.8.604-07). Tamora and Doris have drunk from the cup of wrath Doris wishes on Mariam (4.8.600); Tamora and Doris represent the male definition of the contaminated maternal body.

Doris signifies all women who are interchangeable in the male world, just as Tamora and Lavinia are interchangeable in *Titus Andronicus*. As absent signifiers, Doris and Mariam, like all women in the ancient Judaic patriarchy, are considered to be *nought* or nothing. Being *nought* is figurative decapitation. Cary uses this word several times in the drama. The status of Doris and Mariam as nought is directly related to the homonym *naught*, referring to women's connection to Eve and the original sin. Being free or appearing to be free from *naught* also decapitates women and makes them *nought*, purified entities.

Sohemus suggests that Mariam's vow to foreswear the bed of her husband is unwise, but that Mariam will not listen to his advice, which she considers to be *nought* (3.3.144). Male language is becoming unimportant to Mariam. This section of the play is directly related to the Chorus's profession that a spotless woman must free herself from naught, from even the suspicion of wrongdoing (3.3.217). Cary may have been influenced in this section of the play by Stefano Guazzo's work or the conduct manuals of her time that reflected sentiments similar to that of those in Guazzo's writing (Ferguson and Weller): "It is not sufficient to be honest and innocent in deed, if she doe not likewise avoyde all suspicion (in respect of the world) between being naught and being thought naught" (165). Herod believes that "Nought is so fix'd, but peevishness may move" (4.3.149). Anger changes the condition of *nought*. Nought is not a fixed term but can be manipulated or changed by male society's edicts.

The concepts of *nought* and *naught* are connected to the women in Shakespeare's plays in William Carroll's analysis: "A woman is not a virgin [or chaste] whose knot is nought because she has been naught" (297). Carroll's word play is significant to Shakespeare and Cary's establishment of Lavinia and Mariam as absent signifiers. The use of *knot/nought/naught* signifies the bond of marriage, the frailty of feminine status in society, and the arbitrary male tenets women must abide by. The very stigma that some of the characters hope to achieve (like the rape of Lavinia by Demetrius and Chiron or Salome's slander of Mariam to persuade Herod to execute Mariam) is also the very aspect of Lavinia and Mariam that not only brings about their downfall but also the disruption of male discourse. Lavinia and Mariam's courage in the face of a fate worse than death and the female body as the mythos of victim display the opposite of *nought*; *nought* is transformed into a text concerning figurative decapitation. Constabarus describes Salome: "You are with nought but wickedness indued" (4.6.346). Tamora and Salome's *knots* of chastity are also *nought* because they have been *naught*, but the opposite result occurs. Tamora and Salome's indiscretions ultimately contribute to their figurative decapitation, make them more sexually objectified, in comparison to the textual disgorgement created by Shakespeare and Cary through the depiction of Lavinia and Mariam.

Because Mariam embodies living death, she is an absent signifier. An example of Mariam's living death appears in the exposition. Before act 1 opens, before Josephus spares Mariam's life, Mariam was waiting for death due to Herod's edict (1.1.50). Mariam lives with the threat of death throughout the play and is finally sentenced to death by her husband in act 4. In addition, Herod's vacillation (4.4.241-58) between killing and imprisoning Mariam emphasizes her *entredeux* status as an absent signifier. Another way in which Mariam is presented as absent signifier is in Mariam's frequent reference to herself in third person; this linguistic effect creates another form of living death. Mariam's use of third person throughout the play foreshadows her execution in act 5 and at the same time defines the existence of women who live under male oppression as a living death. In act 1, scene 2, Mariam states: "Not to be empress of aspiring Rome, / Would Mariam like to Cleopatra live: / With purest body will I press my tomb, / And wish no favours Anthony could give" (199-202). Mariam makes herself a separate entity by speaking about herself in third person. She is the voice of Cary, the voice of all women who are all absent signifiers. She is also the maternal body since she is the mother of children, and in act 5 she returns to the womb/tomb of mother earth in death. Mariam speaks about herself in third person in three other instances: in 3.3, when she tells Sohemus that Mariam will break her own heart before she will break her vow to forego Herod's bed (136); in 4.3, where she discards worldly possessions in preparation for death (109-16); and again in 4.8, where Mariam says, "Who sees for truth that Mariam is untrue?" (581).

Salome also enables the figurative and literal decapitation of Mariam; in act 4, Salome describes Mariam's beauty as an entrapment of men's souls (7.401-02). Salome suggests that Mariam is immodest because she does not blush due to her sins that Salome defines as Mariam's seductive use of her physical beauty (4.7.405). Salome surmises that "Beauty is a blast" (3.1.20). It is like a puff of wind; it is insignificant just as women signify nothingness in the ancient Judaic patriarchy. Beauty also does not last; an old or ugly woman in the patriarchy has lost market value. Salome is analyzing the figurative decapitation of women as simply beautified objects. Eroticizing the female head extends the woman as body or flesh; therefore, the female head becomes a sexual organ, part of female genitals (Eilberg-Schwartz and Doniger 2). The head becomes submerged; it disappears into the body. The female face, eyes, voice, mouth, hair are all part of the erotic experience. Figurative decapitation incorporates the female head into language and societal tenets as just one more part of the female body, an eroticized object to pleasure men. Therefore, female beauty in face and body is a sexual possession to be marketed and manipulated by men.

Cary discusses the fact that women are the object of the gaze by emphasizing the face and facial beauty in her play. Cary ridicules the importance of beauty in male-governed society by comparing the beauty of Mariam to the other female characters: the aging beauty of Doris, the dark beauty of Salome, and the empowered beauty of Cleopatra. All of these women have their own unique beauty, but the male characters in the play only see beauty as a part of women that men own and manipulate to their advantage. Makeup to enhance the beauty of the face as well as words, the *paintings* of women, are also subsumed into the body's text as part of sexual allure. Salome explains this phenomenon when she says of Mariam: "She speaks a beauteous language, but within / Her heart is false as powder: and her tongue / Doth but allure the auditors to sin, / And is the instrument to do you wrong" (4.7.429-32).

Mariam's tongue is part of her beauty, but it is also her chaos. It is explosive. From Salome's viewpoint, Mariam's words enchant men, put them under a spell (4.7.436). In Cary's drama, the abuse of women is provoked by the *sins* of the female characters. Salome's sins are disobedience and unchastity, but Cary wishes to illustrate that in the

Early Modern English patriarchy Mariam's sin is greater: she cannot keep silent. The woman's tongue is identified by the patriarchy as the female phallus, as Lynda Boose explains: "A discourse that locates the tongue as the body's 'unruly member' situates female speech as a symbolic relocation of the male organ, an unlawful appropriation of phallic authority" (263).

Herod discusses the power of Mariam's beauty in act 4.7: "For on the brow of Mariam hangs a fleece (like that in Greek myth), / Whose slenderest twine is strong enough to bind / The hearts of kings" (413-15). This reference connects Mariam's hair to her seductive powers. However, Cary counters the decapitating effect of Herod's comparison in act 4 by connecting Mariam to myth in this statement, thereby giving Mariam's life a more weighty significance. Lavinia in Shakespeare's *Titus Andronicus* is compared to legendary women for the same textual purpose. Salome describes Mariam's hair as a net or bait to "catch the hearts" (4.7.417-18) of men. Cary places a truncated line concerning Mariam's hair near the mention of Mariam as myth and as seductress: "In sooth, I thought it had been hair" (4.7.422). The use of decapitated lines in Cary's drama is another way to underscore or give extra significance to the dramatist's words, or in this case to ridicule the importance of female beauty. Cary turns the sarcasm of Herod's words to Salome about the powers of Mariam's hair back on itself, implying that the oppression that accompanies idealizing women's bodies is a ludicrous enterprise. Set side by side to lines of metrical similarity, the truncated lines disrupt the order of the meter.

Beauty is used as a form of silencing. Graphina enables her own oppression in act 2; when Pheroras suggests that her silence is a sign of female chaos (2.1.42), she refutes his comments by falling in with the party line: "If I be silent, 'tis no more but fear / That I should say too little when I speak: / But since you will my imperfections bear, / In spite of doubt I will my silence break" (2.1.52). Graphina says exactly what she knows Pheroras wants to hear. She is contrasted with Salome, who says exactly what no one wants to hear, and with

Mariam, who speaks when she should not and refuses to speak when her speech is elicited. Pheroras, Graphina's intended, anatomizes his love (3.1.15-18) in the manner of a Petrarchan blazon that figuratively decapitates the object of desire.

In like manner, the male characters in the play often figuratively decapitate and re-construct Mariam as the epitome of purity through the use of the Petrarchan blazon. Constabarus defines "sweet-faced Mariam, as free from guilt / As Heaven from spots" (1.6.487-88); Mariam is one who was destined, by Herod's edict, to be of "purest blood [. . .] unjustly spilt" (489). Mariam is compared to the sun in act 4 (1.8-9) and her face is described as cheering Herod's heart (4.1.12). Herod relates that Mariam's eyes are like stars (4.4.220), she brings light to the world (4.4.236), she is "the flaming sun" (4.7.395) and "the moon" (4.7.396), and "her forehead is like the sky" (4.7.451). Mariam's speech is "world-amazing wit" (4.7.428). In act 5, Herod depicts Mariam as a "precious mirror made by wonderous art" (1.125) that "dazzl'd" (5.1.124) Herod's eye and that he keeps folded in his heart (5.1.127). Mariam is a mirror in which Herod sees his own reflection. She is also a prisoner of Herod's heart.

Even at the end of *The Tragedy of Mariam*, Herod and Nuntio continue to discuss the executed Mariam, not as a subject, but as a series of objectified parts: her "rare" beauty and hands (5.1.153-54) and her "fair" face and virtuous nature (5.1.198). Herod uses Petrarchan discourse in a futile attempt to restructure Mariam after she has been executed. He states that Mariam's hands were whiter than snow (5.1.151). Lavinia's hands are a signifying presence in *Titus Andronicus* also; Herod sees Mariam's hands but not what they represent about her: her generosity and love that Herod took advantage of and her innocence that Herod refuses to believe when he has her executed. Herod's use of Petrarchan discourse *decapitates* Mariam figuratively just as she is literally decapitated in that same section of the play.

Cary uses body parts as figurative language in her drama, especially repetition of the ear, mouth, and tongue, female body parts that men try to censor. She intends to show through these repetitive references the difference between the Petrarchan blazon that dissects women into body parts and her textual use of such parts to create a subtext of disgorgement. For example, Herod connects Mariam's chastity to her public speech: "She's unchaste, / Her mouth will ope to ev'ry stranger's ear" (4.7.433-34). Patriarchal society sees public conversation on the part of women as a sign of unchaste behavior that needs to be controlled; on the other hand, a woman of magnanimous spirit might be described in like manner with no derogatory emphasis.

The question of rape, another form of figurative decapitation through the manipulation of female sexuality, is broached by Cary through Mariam's relationship to Herod. The execution of Mariam at Herod's order is a violation, a figurative rape of her since Mariam will not sexually yield to Herod voluntarily as Jocelyn Catty asserts (160). I agree with her assessment that throughout the play there are images of women's sexual vulnerability clashing with images of their sexual power (161). Once Mariam chooses to forego Herod's bed, she chooses execution rather than to be raped by her husband. Years after Mariam's death, Herod is reported in historical documents to have entered the sepulchre where Mariam was interred and removed gold furniture and precious goods so that he could pay his debts (Ferguson and Weller 166). By violating her tomb, Herod enacts Mariam's rape. In act 4, Herod says he will violate "holy David's sepulchre" (4.3.105) and "make the Temple bare" (4.3.108) if Mariam wants wealth to make her happy. Through these words, he violates the maternal body, the site of the womb/tomb, since as Adelman observes, the womb of the maternal body represents birth and death. The patriarchal fear of castration by the monstrous mother (257) is the agent that produces chaos. This chaos dates back to birth, "the sin of origin," where a child is contaminated by the female body and is born only to die (267).

Constabarus's bitter diatribe on female sinfulness (4.6.311-50) is another example of how words can wound.

Not only can words be used to violate women, but Cary utilizes various manifestations of breath, the force behind words, as examples of the decapitation of women. Salome accuses Alexandra and Mariam of spending "suppliant breath" to plot to separate from Herod. Salome envisions the two women as triumphant in Herod's death, moving on to find another male conquest (1.3.207-10). In this sentence, Salome twists the generosity of Christian humility depicted as breath into a form of female decapitation by men that women are happy to be released from. Women must behave with humility in ancient Judaic culture because they need men to take care of them. However, breath is lost or "spent" in suppliance according to Salome. Salome also suggests that Mariam feigns this behavior while she actually has a hidden agenda to manipulate men. Salome is projecting her own manipulative powers of verbal and bodily persuasion, a reverse decapitation or castration of men, on Mariam who does not use Salome's tactics.

Mariam also relates Herod's commands and edicts to breath in act 3 (3.191). In 2.2, Babas's first son fears, as Mariam does in other sections of the drama, that Herod's "breath will be preserv'd to make a number bleed" (2.2.149-50). This statement foreshadows the outcome of his life and Mariam's. Herod's breath decapitates the other characters figuratively and literally. The breath and voice of men fill the temple with the news of Herod's life or "rebirth" (3.2.38); Herod is not dead as everyone believed. This is an example of male characters in the play usurping the birthing process from the maternal body. In essence, Herod gives birth to himself, using the church as midwife, resurrecting himself from the dead. Salome, however, is incredulous of the church's ability and the power of language to usurp female birthright: "What? Can your news restore my brother's breath?" (3.2.42). Just as Cary creates a disgorgement by using the repetition of female body parts as a subversion of the blazon, Cary also disgorges by subverting Herod and Salome's "breath" through Mariam's "loosing" of breath in act 5.

Male sense of exclusion, male fear of female power over life and death through giving birth, leads men, like Herod in Cary's play, to decapitate women figuratively and sometimes literally. Men in ancient Jerusalem decapitate by bridling women with a network of propaganda; they attempt to control female biology, to be the masters of language and voice. These men who try to take control of female sexuality feel empowered, because they have usurped female birthright. The seizing and manipulation of birthright is of central importance to Herod's ascent in the political hierarchy due to his marriage to Mariam. Herod surveys Rome in much the same way he describes Mariam (4.1.22); both are the objects of his desire (4.1.35) The male characters in the play envision their ownership of land, fortunes, and status just as they see their possession of women. Herod manipulates Mariam's identity in an attempt to ally himself with her family, to legitimize himself. More than once in the play, Herod and his family are referred to as "base" Edomites (1.2.84), as "damned Esau's" heirs (1.2.84), who do not have the claim to royal blood that Mariam does.

Herod does not actually appear until act 4; Cary suggests here that the decapitating force of the ancient Judaic patriarchy does not need to be bodily present to have influence. Herod twists words when he speaks to Mariam. His words are indicated to woo and convince her that she controls him when Herod is fully aware that Mariam has been imprisoned as his wife for years. "To be by thee directed I will woo / For in thy pleasure lies my highest pride" (4.3.99-100). There is no bisexuality of discourse when Herod speaks; Mariam's "pleasure" is violated by Herod's "pride."

Herod uses language to cajole Mariam out of her mood so that she will take him back into her bed. Herod has used wooing words with Mariam before when he wanted to win Mariam as a replacement for his wife, Doris. "Thine [Mariam's] eye / Is pure as Heaven, but impure thy mind" (4.4.190-91). This disparity between mind (male text) and body (female text) is a major issue in the play and part of the figurative decapitation of women by male society. In contrast, Mariam is not able to disconnect her body and her thoughts. Later, Herod intimates that "a beauteous body hides a loathsome soul" (4.4.178); the soul and the body are disconnected for him as well.

In 4.4, Herod attempts to control Mariam's sexuality by confronting her when he suspects a liaison between Mariam and Sohemus, who is supposed to be guarding Mariam against any intruder. Mariam's reply is terse: "They can tell that say I lov'd him, Mariam says not so" (4.4.193-94). Herod would rather hear Mariam plotted to kill him than to find out she has been unfaithful (4.4.207). Herod's jealousy decapitates Mariam and instigates her imprisonment and scrutiny of her by guards while he is away. She has protested her innocence to the charges of infidelity earlier in the play (1.3.258), which is confirmed by Salome's husband, Constabarus (1.6.487-92). Adultery is a central issue in the texts of patriarchal societies.

In four polemical tracts, Milton addressed Mosaic divorce law, a subject Cary discusses from an opposing subject position in *Mariam*, as Shari A. Zimmerman examines (554). Cary's discussion of divorce through her character, Salome, in 1.4, is purposefully contrasted to her depiction of Mariam, another woman in an unhappy marriage, who, unlike Salome, seeks death rather than divorce. Therefore, divorce is a controversial issue that Cary disputes in her drama. The controversy of female adultery and promiscuity is connected to the issue of divorce. Salome does not understand why the bible is so narrow in focus; she feels women should be able to divorce their spouses just as men are allowed to do (1.4.303-10 and 1.6.419), voicing the opinion of Cary who was herself in an unhappy union. Constabarus chides Salome by telling her that from Moses's day until the present, 1400 years have passed but there has never been a woman who divorced a man (1.6.437-52). In other words, a married woman is indebted to and possessed by her husband. Marriage is a system of returns for men;

the woman's obedience to her husband is the return. If debts are paid, balance and order resume. In this system, words end in a balance, in a reduction to a binary system of language. Women are either chaste or adulterous. In the case of Cary's play, the accused adulterer is Mariam. However, Mariam's death does not bring balance back to the system.

Herod believes that words and oaths are important parts of male power (4.4.172, 174). He does not want to hear a word from Sohemus when he orders his death in act 4 but cannot hear enough about Mariam's words in death from Nuntio in act 5. Herod privileges Mariam's words over her bodily text. When Herod thinks Mariam intended to poison him, he names her "painted devil / [. . .] white enchantress" (4.4.175 76), connecting Mariam's supposed actions to the evil of Eve's original sin in Eden. Herod claims Mariam is so foul that she cannot be cleaned (4.4.176-77). This is the fate of women who fall out of favor with male society. In the binary system of Herod's language, "love and hate do fight" (4.4.244).

The male gaze that figuratively decapitates women is described by Nuntio in act 5 as the "gazing troop" (1.21) who looked on Mariam's death. Herod believes he has power over *history* and *herstory*, in fact, over all stories (5.1.47); he claims that he will "smother" any record of Alexandra except that her name will live in infamy (5.1.48). Herod, as representative of the patriarchy of Jerusalem, believes that he has control over all texts or discourses. However, Mariam's "silent prayer" (5.1.84) right before her death undermines his attempt and is her expression of *herstory* that overthrows *history*. It is also apparent that Herod adores Mariam for her name and status that she brings to him in the Jewish hierarchy, but he is not really in love with her (5.1.70). In fact, he attempts to consume her text into himself so that no one else can have contact with it: "Each word she said / Shall be the food whereon my heart is fed" (5.1.71-72). Words have more power over Herod than the significant statement Mariam's bodily text in death has made. Nuntio resists Herod's attempts to change Mariam's text at the scaffold by controlling Nuntio's words (5.1.94).

Herod believes he can control language as well as women; he tells Mariam that he will exile "all unkind conceits" (4.3.144) if Mariam will smile. "My word, though not my sword, made Mariam bleed" (5.1.189) and Cain, standing in for Herod, "stain'd the virgin earth with brother's blood" (5.1.250); Herod believes that the power of language, the power of constructs figuratively decapitates and is stronger than the power of the phallus and the maternal body. The word has taken over the maternal body's text, the birthing or productive powers of Mariam. Also, the maternal body as "virgin earth" is stained with blood by man, rather than the maternal body staining her progeny with blood through birth; Herod is taking over the power of birthing through the use of language. In fact, he attempts to conquer Mariam in death and reinscribe his text on her by using a great many words (5.1.153-258), but to no avail.

In essence, Herod violates the site of the maternal body linguistically by trying to take possession of Mariam, the mother of his children, with his words. He defiles this site in the same way he defiled Doris by abandoning her and by violating Mariam's body through ordering her execution. In reality, Herod's power in the hierarchy has not afforded him the power to produce life, but instead, he is the harbinger of death for those within his sphere of influence: Mariam, Aristobulus, Hircanus, Josephus, Constabarus, and Babas's sons. The maternal body gives the breath of life to its progeny, but the patriarchies of ancient Rome and Judea as well as Early Modern England attempt to smother the mother. As Salome puts it, the female womb is a room that men take possession of (1.4.318).

"By three days hence, if wishes could revive, / I know himself would make me oft alive" (5.1.77-78). Mariam understands that after her death, Herod will feel remorse and attempt to reconstruct her, just as Lavinia's family tries to do to her after her rape and mutilation, but the male world is unable to linguistically resurrect these two women.

Herod says the very thing Mariam foretells: "Is there no trick to make her breathe again?" (5.1.89). Later, he reveals his belief that "there might be found by art / Strange way of cure; 'tis sure rare things are done / By an inventive head, and willing heart" (5.1.91-93). In the case of Mariam and Lavinia, the men in their lives think they can bring these women back to their original state, that somehow they can re-order the universe so that everything is whole and unified again, but their words and actions are futile. Nuntio parallels Herod's inability to reconstruct Mariam with male ineptness to resurrect "holy Abraham" (5.1.96) from entombment. Herod again tries to resurrect Mariam when he denies that she is dead: "But sure she is not dead, you [Nuntio] did but jest" (5.1.135).

Through marriage, Herod has kept Mariam, like Babas's sons, in a "living tomb" (2.2.117), "quick buried" (2.2.120) and "confin'd" (2.2.121). Herod has controlled Mariam's identity by murdering the support group of kinsmen around her (1.2.81) to usurp their right to the Jewish monarchy, manipulated Mariam sexually through the legitimacy controversy of her children versus Doris's offspring (1.2.137), suppressed Mariam through marriage while expecting her to exhibit the attributes of a submissive wife, and effectively stopped her honest speech through death (5.1.90). Mariam's tragedy is the tragedy of all women repressed by patriarchal dominance into silence.

Disgorgement

> I have volcanoes on my lands. But no lava: what wants to flow is breath. And not just any old way. The breath wants a form. 'Write me!' [. . .] The nature of its fury demanded the form that stops the least, the body without a frame, without skin, without walls, the flesh that doesn't dry, doesn't stiffen, doesn't clot the wild blood that wants to stream through it. (Cixous, "Coming to Writing" 10)

Cary refers to breath in many different ways in *The Tragedy of Mariam*; breath in the epigraph represents figurative and literal decapitation as well as a disgorgement of the female body's text without the framing effects of figurative decapitation. Cary creates a signification of the female body by using the verbal and bodily texts of her female characters in various ways. In fact, each female character emphasizes a different aspect of Cary's textual disgorgement, but Mariam is the embodiment of all forms of disgorgement in the play: an *entredeux* text, a subversive discourse, a merging of discourses, a text of generosity, and an absent signifier. For example, Cary uses Mariam and her *entredeux* status as an absent signifier in death to disgorge.

Mariam is Cary's subversion of male constructs like the blazon. Mariam thought her face and her virtue, the Petrarchan objectification of herself and her obedience to female attributes dictated by the ancient Judaic patriarchy, were enough to save her (4.8.559-62), but she realizes in 4.8 that the power of her beauty and her chastity is not as substantial as the power of her breath, Cary's representation of the soul. Another form of Cary's disgorgement appears in her use of the word "breath"; Mariam's "looks alone preserved your sovereign's [Herod's] breath" (4.4.254). In this statement, Mariam's looks are joined to Herod's breath in a bisexuality of discourse. Breath represents Cary's disgorgement of generosity and service related to Mariam (3.3.214), and breath is connected to the expression of love between Mariam and Herod (4.4.218). Mariam, like Lavinia in *Titus Andronicus*, is an absent signifier, a symbol of chaos and living death that disables and merges with various constructs. Mariam is literally decapitated in act 5, and the act of beheading her is totally devoted to revealing her body as text. By having Mariam's head severed from her body (1.90), Cary creates a character that is all bodily text.

"Tell thou my lord thou saw'st me loose my breath" (5.1.73). These are part of Mariam's last words before her beheading. In the Ferguson and Weller edition of Cary's drama, line 73 has 'loose', but in other versions, like the Cerasano and Davies edition of Cary's text, the spelling is 'lose.' It is my contention that Cary intended to use the word "loose" at this important part of the drama. The "loosing" of breath is Mariam's chaos; it is her way of deconstructing the hierarchy and its hold on her. The "loosing" of breath is a figurative vomiting, a refusal to choke down the life of oppression Mariam has been forced to live. The paradox here is that though commanded to speak to prove their virtue, speaking on the scaffold negated virtuousness for women in the patriarchy, as Lisa Jardine points out (109). Cary uses the "loosing" of breath as well as Mariam's terse last words to outpour an expression of innocence in the face of tyranny.

The loss of breath is connected to Herod in 1.1, and to Mariam in 5.1; these sections frame the drama. Breath is connected to the hypocrisy of speech in 1.1, of wanting triumph over and death of the oppressor: "When Herod liv'd, that now is done to death, / Oft have I wish'd that I from him were free: / Oft have I wish'd that he might lose his breath, / Oft have I wish'd his carcass dead to see" (15-18). Cary uses the word 'lose' to contrast Mariam's wish that Herod "lose" his breath in 1.1 with the death of Mariam in 5.1 in which she "looses" her breath. When Herod is "resurrected" in the play, Mariam considers death as an alternative to continuing to live under her husband's rule. Also, she uses a different word to discuss Herod's death versus her own: Herod "loses" his breath in her dreams of being free of containment in act 1, but when Mariam is on the scaffold in act 5, she takes control of her own life by letting her breath "loose," triumphing over her husband's tyranny. Moreover, Mariam will not get into a game of words with Herod; her words in act 5 are terse. Therefore, breath becomes synonymous not only with objectification but also with language.

Subversion and Chaos Through Language

> She must write her self, because this is the invention of a *new insurgent* writing which, when the moment of her liberation has come, will allow her to carry out the indispensable ruptures and transformations in her history. (Cixous, "Laugh" 880)

In the narrative, Mariam's life and death "rupture" the world that Herod is trying to maintain and the texts that he inflicts upon her. Mariam is given positive and negative attributes by Cary in an attempt to rewrite scriptural history; in addition, Cary "transforms" past history concerning women through the veiled discourse of her closet drama and uses her writing as a re-telling, a myth-making in process, to mask and give voice to her own life story, to "write her self." Mariam is constructed as arrogant and prideful (1.3.235-38) but also generous (1.2.134) and innocent (4.6.312-14). Her pride is evident in her haughtiness towards Salome, Herod's sister in Cary's play (1.3.223-26 and 233-38). Cary could be haughty about her genealogy, as Ferguson and Weller discuss, but also faithful to her husband and to her religious beliefs (3.193, 195).

The male characters in the play place Mariam in the binary system of language: she must be either virtuous or unchaste. Her verbal and bodily text undermines their attempts to construct her, because her traits are *entredeux*. Mariam's character is transgressive and destabilizes the dichotomy of woman as either virgin or whore. Her words deconstruct the concepts of females as property and female propriety. By engineering her own death, Mariam refuses to be Herod's property. Her improprieties are her unguarded speech to any man other than Herod which he views as "adultery," her vows to keep Herod from her bed, and her inflammatory words to Salome about the latter's family heritage.

The Chorus explains about Mariam, "'Tis not so glorious for her to be free, / As by her proper self restrain'd to be" (3.3.220). Cary splits the word 'herself' with the word 'proper' (Ferguson and Weller 165). The dramatist is disrupting the social relationship between women and men; she is discussing appropriate behavior as designated by men for women, as well as women as male property. Mariam's speech and behavior in the play subvert the ideas of what is proper for women in a society that views them as the property of men. Mariam's speech undermines the societal constructs about women's speech practices. In her play, Cary "negotiates and recasts the attendant contingencies upon women's utterance" (Catty 131) by creating a dialogue with texts written during the pamphlet wars and with conduct manuals for women from the Early Modern era in England. Cary's play engages with the debate on female speech in private and public settings. Many women writers in the Early Modern period responded to attacks on women such as the one in Gosenhill's *Schoolhouse of Women*. Cary's drama, like Jane Anger's *Protection for Women* written in 1589, speaks out against the oppression of women by male society.

If a woman speaks out in a patriarchal culture, she is considered unchaste because she is usurping the place of men. In 1.1, Mariam begins by stating: "How oft have I with public voice run on / To censure Rome's last hero for deceit" (1 2). Mariam's outspokenness is criticized by Sohemus, who believes that "Unbridled speech is Mariam's worst disgrace" (3.3.183). In her research of the Early Modern English practice of bridling, Lynda Boose illustrates that women who were deemed scolds or shrews could be disciplined by having their mouths bridled with iron bits or gags (267). Mariam's "unbridled speech" undermines male constructs that dictate female silence. The Chorus reiterates Sohemus's concern about Mariam's speech: "For in a wife it is no worse to find, / A common body than a common mind" (3.3.243-44). The central question in *The Tragedy of Mariam* is "a wife's right to speak," according to Catherine Belsey, "to a position from which to protest" (171). A woman who speaks threatens the difference of the sexes. The female characters in Cary's play produce speech in various forms: Alexandra's speech is chaotic, Cleopatra's image is muted by Alexandra's distortion of her, Doris's rhetoric is venomous, Salome's words are veiled subversion, and Graphina's words are submissive.

Mariam's subversion of discourse is different from Lavinia's in *Titus Andronicus*. Lavinia's bodily text undermines the constructs of male society that dictate women to be silent, obedient and chaste. Lavinia's mutilated form is silent because she has no tongue, obedient because she has no hands, and chaste due to her sexual ruination through rape. According to the men in her life Mariam is not silent, obedient, or chaste due to her "unbridled speech" (3.3.183), but she is so at the time of her death. Before her execution, she is silent, she is obedient during the moments leading to her execution, but more importantly she is obedient to her own beliefs, and she is chaste because she foregoes Herod's bed, taking control of her body. Mariam goes to her death believing that the freedom to express forthright speech, to have unencumbered access to voice, is more important to the female body than royal bloodline and physical beauty.

"For he, by barring me from liberty, / To shun my ranging, taught me first to range" (1.1. 25-26). Mariam's word play on the word 'range' deconstructs the binary opposition of the hart/heart hunt, the game/dogs, stag/doe (all of these opposing terms descriptive of Herod and Mariam's relationship). Lavinia in *Titus Andronicus* is referred to as a *doe* by the men who oppress her. Mariam uses the word 'range' to delineate that she is a prisoner as Herod's wife due to his jealousy which has changed her feelings about constancy towards her husband in her "ranging" speech. Mariam's opening words that Herod's possession of her has taught her to "range" are ironically opposed by Herod's text stating that "no creature having her, can wish to range" (4.7.484). Herod's oppression taught Mariam about her own desire for freedom; she says, "virgin freedom left me unrestrained" (1.1.72). However, Mariam realizes that she will never be free.

In act 5, Nuntio's translation of Mariam's bodily text in death is an assault on Herod's ears (1.99), a violation of the order of the hierarchy. Nuntio administers and Herod hears Mariam's text as an assault on everything an androcentric society believes in. Mariam divorces herself from tales of slander through her death (5.1.114), a deconstruction of male texts. "My punishment must needs sufficient be, / In missing that content I valued most" (5.1.116-17). Cary has created layered meanings in this line of Herod's. Herod not only admits that Mariam's life contented him and that he will be punished since now she no longer can be a companion to him. Herod also misses the opportunity to try to make Mariam content with her life with him.

However, the word 'content' can also mean the purport of text. Therefore, Herod has inscribed Mariam with his own text; he will miss the content of her verbal and bodily discourse now that she is dead. The word 'missing' also has more than one context here. Herod misses the point that Mariam will never be contented with him. Also, Herod misses the point of the content of Mariam's bodily text in life and in death, something that he "values" and therefore tries to possess but also something that he does not really comprehend.

Nuntio claims that Mariam's bodily text through her death in act 5 is "the last of her that was the best" (1.22). Language has no power over the chaos of bodily text in death; words cannot explain or rename Mariam: "All tongues suffice not her sweet name to raise" (5.1.32). Alexandra uses the chaos of her discourse to attempt to darken Mariam's bodily text as Mariam goes to the scaffold by "loudly railing" (5.1.36) at her daughter, but Alexandra's words are powerless over the body's text. Alexandra even goes so far as to renounce Mariam's birth; she turns her back on her own maternity (5.1.43-44). Herod wants to be able to control the chaos of his own words, his sentence of execution, as well as Mariam's text created through death, but this is impossible: "Oh, that I could that sentence now control" (5.1.74). 'Sentence' has two meanings here. Herod is unable to contain the chaos, the deconstructive force of the female body's text that he let loose by having Mariam put to death.

Graphina's name means 'writing' in Greek; Cary expresses herself through translating the female body's text into writing. Lavinia in *Titus Andronicus* embodies the idea of communication through writing as well. In act 3, Salome denigrates writing through the figure of Graphina; Salome constructs her as being "of meaner mind" (3.1.12) with "natural defects" (3.1.13). Cary implies that only the body's text is the purest form of expression, exploring her own imprisonment in writing plays for private consumption versus writing dramas for public production. Public production is created by using the body as text since the body is the actor's instrument. Cary also addresses the issue of women's public versus private speech in act 1 when she has Mariam in the first scene speak to herself in private but, as Ferguson and Weller point out, since the character is appearing onstage, she is also speaking in public through soliloquy, using the body as text (152).

Jouissance through Bisexual Discourse

> Writing is the passageway, the entrance, the exit, the dwelling place of the other in me. (Cixous, *The Newly Born Woman* 85)

The female characters in Cary's play are absent signifiers; they are insignificant presences because they are depicted as women living in a patriarchal society, but even so, they are capable of signifying, capable of subverting language, capable of transforming their absence into a beginning or continuation of presence. Cary's characters use their marginalization to their advantage. Cary signifies through her writing. Therefore, the joining of absence with signification creates a bisexuality of discourse, a link between figurative decapitation and textual disgorgement, connecting the silencing of women with the signifying practices of male-governed society.

Doris is an absent signifier; she experiences the lack of her rightful place at Herod's side that she believes has been usurped by Mariam. Doris's progeny also have been displaced by Mariam's in the societal hierarchy. However, Doris is still in the background, waiting to step in when and if Mariam is displaced. Doris is significant because Herod could reinstate Doris and Antipater to their former status if he grew weary of Mariam. Mariam is the subject of Doris and Antipater's dialogue in 2.3. Because Mariam is the title character of the drama, she is often the main subject of a scene in the play even when she is absent. When Herod returns in act 4, she is the main topic of conversation between Herod and Pheroras, Herod and the Butler, and

Herod and Salome. Mariam is the center of the discussion once again in act 5 between Herod and Nuntio. Pheroras explains Mariam's absent significance in this manner: "Absent use of her fair name I make" (4.2.70). Pheroras is using Mariam's name to manipulate Herod into killing Constabarus so that Salome can marry Silleus.

Cary's use of apostrophe in 1.1 (5-8), situates Mariam's dialogue as linguistic intercourse with a male absent signifier, in this case, Julius Caesar. The use of apostrophe creates an imaginary interchange between two absent signifiers: the figure addressed in the apostrophe and a woman. Mariam also addresses her grandsire, Hircanus, in apostrophe in 1.1 (43-46). In this section, Hircanus is an absent signifier because he was executed by Herod but has not been forgotten by Mariam and her mother. In the last act, Nuntio's opening comments (5.1.1-4) are a dialogue with Mariam in apostrophe, a merging with the female body's text.

Nuntio's discourse that relates Mariam's death to Herod is a bisexuality of discourse. Nuntio is a male creation of Cary's who speaks in her place; his speech is connected to hers and transformed by hers. Nuntio's text is also connected to Mariam's bodily text in death. In act 5, Cary has Mariam designate Nuntio to be the narrator of her text (1.60). Nuntio explains that he is the "relator of [Mariam's] end, / The end of beauty, chastity, and wit" (1.3-4), that Mariam's bodily text exudes these qualities. Herod is vulnerable to an attack of words (5.1.16). Herod misguidedly believes that Nuntio has usurped Herod's position as the one who inscribes meaning on Mariam: "Thou [Nuntio] dost usurp my right, my tongue was fram'd / To be the instrument of Mariam's praise" (5.1.29-30). However, Herod is in error; Nuntio does not inscribe meaning on Mariam. Nuntio is simply the translator of Mariam's text into language. *The Tragedy of Mariam* is about the joining of power and desire, the power of Mariam's verbal chaos that expresses the dramatist's desire to disgorge.

Herod's deluded perception of Mariam's "unbridled" desire brings them to the scaffold in act 5; as Jennifer Louise Heller articulates, when a woman transgresses boundaries, her "inner desires become suspect. But these desires are inevitably located in a space that cannot be known [. . .] a woman cannot provide irrefutable 'proof' of her inner desires, no matter what evidence she may offer" (426). Cary's textual disgorgement, however, does makes Mariam's desires "known" and Cary's desires as well, and in so doing, creates a textual *jouissance*. For *The Tragedy of Mariam* is about the joining of power and desire, the power of Mariam's verbal chaos that expresses the dramatist's desire to disgorge.

Conclusion

> Without him she'd remain in a state of distressing and distressed undifferentiation, unbordered, unorganized, 'unpoliced' by the phallus...incoherent, chaotic, and embedded in the Imaginary in her ignorance of the Law of the Signifier. Without him she would in all probability not be contained by the threat of death, might, even perhaps, believe herself eternal, immortal [. . .] she's the unorganizable feminine construct. (Cixous, "Castration" 168)

Mariam is Cary's creation of an "unorganizable feminine construct." Mariam is not "contained by the threat of death." Her choice of literal decapitation rather than bearing her own figurative decapitation any longer is Cary's subversive finale. Mariam's death is aligned with references to breath throughout the drama. Constabarus describes Salome's fickle behavior in act 2: "As good go hold the wind as make her stay" (2.4.323). This sentence can also be applied to Mariam who lets loose her breath or spirit in death; her breath of life is like the wind that cannot be contained. It is an outpouring of text. Breath is associated with time and with death's chaos (2.4.353-54, 355-56). Breath leaves the body in death (2.4.379-80); therefore breath becomes Mariam's subversion as well as a statement about woman as absent presence.

In 3.3, Mariam makes her decision to depart, to separate from a world of suffering. "Tell me I shall a death disgraceful die, but tell me not that Herod is return'd" (128-29). In act 1, Herod is presumed dead, but now Mariam realizes that report was premature. In 3.3, she sees the hypocrisy in her words in the opening of the play when she mourned Herod's death; she tells Sohemus: "But speak no more to me, in vain ye speak / To live with him I so profoundly hate" (3.3.137-38). Mariam also perceives the truth in Sohemus's words about tempering her behavior in 3.3, but she has made up her mind. She knows the decision she is making will be disruptive. It is here that Mariam begins to engineer her own death, because she sees that only death will free her from oppression. Monique Wittig in *Les Guérillères* says that if women are possessed by men as currency, as items of exchange, as merchandise for bartering, then "what belongs to you [women] on this earth? Only death. No power on earth can take that away from you [. . .] if happiness consists in possession of something, then hold fast to this sovereign happiness – to die" (116). The behavior of Mariam signs her death warrant, and Mariam knows what she is doing. Through death, characters are removed by the dramatist from the order of society and the binary system of language. Through death, Mariam's bodily text becomes public, rather than private.

The connection between face and thoughts is examined in act 4 as Mariam realizes her own complicity – "myself against myself conspir'd" (8.533) – in the objectification of herself. She states: "Am I the Mariam that presum'd so much, / And deem'd my face must needs preserve my breath? / Ay, I it was that thought my beauty such, / As it alone could countermand my death. / Now death will teach me" (4.8.525-29). Mariam discovers that Herod had left orders with Josephus, Herod's uncle, to murder her if he did not return from facing accusations in Rome. She utilizes speech and silence as well as bodily text to create a textual chaos.

In 4.3, Mariam calls Herod a liar (136). With her words she purposefully engineers her death, knowing that subversive speech will get her executed. Cary uses the character of Mariam to reveal "how a woman handles tyranny and maintains her own integrity," as Sandra Fischer asserts (227). In 4.8, Mariam declares that although her body will die, "My soul is free from adversary's power" (569-70). She bids farewell to the earth: "Now earth, farewell, though I be yet but young, / Yet I, methinks, have known thee too too long" (627-28). Herod tells her that "for impurity shall Mariam die" (4.4.192) and that "Hell itself lies hid / Beneath thy heavenly show" (4.4.203-04). The excuse for executing Mariam is that she is impure as well as treasonous; Salome has implicated Mariam in a plan to poison Herod. Herod feels she has consorted with Sohemus and thus become unchaste. Herod describes Mariam as Constabarus defined Salome: Mariam has a "wavering heart" (4.7.510). Herod is inscribing his own text on Mariam. Of course, her "wavering" nature comes from "discontent" (4.7.510). The men in Herod's world cannot abide her subversive text which disrupts the credo for women of being silent, obedient and chaste.

Herod admits that Mariam's bodily text in death will *speak*; therefore, the executioner must be deaf and blind so that he will not be affected by her (4.7.440). "Her eyes can speak, and in their speaking move" (4.7.445). Mariam's bodily text does not encompass order, reason, and hierarchy. Salome fears Herod is losing his grip on reality, that his "thoughts do rave" (4.7.453), so she entreats him to "speak of reason more, of Mariam less" (4.7.456). Salome's words endorse reason and oppose Mariam's text of disorder. The power of Mariam's chaos has affected Herod's words and thoughts; in fact, she has affected Herod so greatly that he will not look at her (4.7.505). Herod describes Mariam's death as the catalyst of a great disturbance that imbalances nature. The balance in the heavens, of the sun and moon, that have before this been "safely governed" (5.1.204) on a "steadfast course" (5.1.206) are now disrupted. The earth is said to rebel at the idea of Mariam's execution (4.7.361-82).

Herod reiterates this idea when he sends Salome to deliver the order for Mariam's death. From Herod's perspective, Salome is thus "gone to bid the world be overthrown" (4.7.390). Salome sees the execution of Mariam as a favorable upheaval, a long overdue re-ordering of the king's household. More importantly, however, Mariam does and says things in the play to "reverse all order" (1.6.458). By executing Mariam, Herod has betrayed his own power (5.1.285), admitting that the power of the female body's text outweighs his own jurisdiction. Frances Dolan explores that idea that the executed female represents male impotence, the inability to control female chaos (166). Female bodily text floods over, overwhelms, and destroys order and unity. Mariam's body is executed but her text continues every time the text of Cary's play is read and studied. The literal decapitation of Mariam does not reinforce the consumption of her voice by her body, which would physically embody her own figurative decapitation, but instead, Mariam's execution releases her voice from the figurative containment of the body.

If masculine commands conflicted with a woman's Christian conscience, conduct books in Early Modern England claimed that the woman had a right to disobey, as Margaret Ferguson discusses (244). Rather than stay with a husband who has murdered her kinsman, Mariam chooses to contrive her own death and reside in heaven in "Sara's [Abraham's wife's] lap" (4.8.574). This admission ties Mariam to the maternal body in death since Sara was believed to be her grandmother. This statement emphasizes matriarchal versus patriarchal descent: the mother's identity was important in Jewish genealogies. Herod admits that "within her [Mariam's] purer veins the blood did run" (5.1.179). Although Herod is referring to his loss of Mariam as his bloodline connection to his social status, the blood of the maternal body is actually what flows through Mariam's veins and her death returns her to this maternal body. Cary disgorges the mother-tongue through Mariam. Herod describes Sara as one who at all ages attracted men (5.1.181), but he just as easily could be describing the maternal body and the mother-tongue this body teaches to its young. Herod laments Mariam's death: "Oh, that her [Sara's] issue had as long been liv'd"

(5.1.182), but the language and law of male-governed society obscure the life of the maternal body's progeny.

Cary extols "virtues of patience, fortitude, and unselfishness" (Beilin, "Elizabeth Cary" 63). Although several of the characters attest to Mariam's purity of spirit and mind (e.g. Sohemus, 3.3.208), Mariam defends her "honour" by discarding all worldly things to purify herself further; she says she must retain her innocence at all costs (3.3.171-80). Herod foolishly thinks Mariam will be happy if she is "empress of Arabia crown'd" (4.3.103), however, Mariam indicates in act 1 that she does not desire fortune, position or social status (2.199-200). In act 4, Mariam's forthright speech is her triumph over the adversity of female life:

> I neither have of power nor riches want,
> I have enough, nor do I wish for more:
> Your offers to my heart no ease can grant,
> Except they could my brother's life restore.
> No, had you wished the wretched Mariam glad,
> Or had your love to her been truly tied:
> Nay had you not desir'd to make her sad,
> My brother nor my grandsire had not died. (4.3.109-16)

At the end of the play, Nuntio refers to the sun's respect of Mariam's death as a metaphoric example of the rise of the phoenix from the ashes (5.1.24). In other words, Mariam's text in death *speaks*. The Chorus predicts that Mariam's death will "draw her story into history" (5.1.290). The statement derived from Mariam's execution is the text of all the female characters and the author of *The Tragedy of Mariam*: the ineffectiveness of male dominion over textual disgorgement.

Mariam's death also has some linguistic parallels to Whitney's poem "The Manner of Her Will." Herod and Nuntio are the witnesses to Mariam's bodily text. Whitney's poem lists pen, paper, ink, and Time as the witnesses to her "will." These are the same implements that bear witness to the *jouissance* of Mariam's bodily discourse. Mariam's blood spilt in execution is her ink, Nuntio is commanded to tell her tale (he becomes the *page* or messenger that carries her tale), Cary as dramatist usurps the pen(is) from men who inscribe women's roles in Early Modern English society by creating the character of Mariam, and Herod tries to control Time, but Mariam's chaos through death disrupts this pursuit. Mariam explains that in three days time after her execution, Herod will try to wish her alive again. Herod restates/reorders her words: "Three days: three hours, three minutes, not so much, / A minute in a thousand part divided; / My penitency for her death is such" (5.1.79-81). However, Herod also realizes Mariam's power to affect Time: "Time runs on, / Her sight can make months minutes, days of weeks" (4.1.17 18). Mariam is linked to the maternal body that has power over Time, over the life and death of her progeny

Cary and Shakespeare use the chaos or fragmentation in relationships, family, and inner selves as a means to disgorge. The fragmented family relationships of Tamora and her two sons and the splintered fighting between the Romans and the Goths catalyze the happenings in *Titus Andronicus*. Lavinia's raped, mutilated, and executed form is a disgorgement because Shakespeare intends to have Lavinia's text inform, and at the same time heal, this disjuncture. Similarly, the domestic problems of Mariam and Herod end at the gallows.

CHAPTER 2
LAVINIA IN WILLIAM SHAKESPEARE'S
TITUS ANDRONICUS

Titus Andronicus discloses a Shakespearean preoccupation with the female body as text. William Shakespeare drafts the character of Lavinia as a figuratively decapitated individual, and through her, he defines *l'écriture féminine* or how a female body speaks its text in a similar manner to Cary's construction of Mariam. Shakespeare thus achieves his disgorgement, a textual manipulation that offsets figurative decapitation's inscription of women's identities. The disgorgement of the female body as text in *Titus Andronicus* is made manifest in the subversion of linguistic constructs and the creation of a figurative *jouissance* through bisexual discourse.

The tragedy in Shakespeare's dramas is that the male characters often misunderstand or misrecognize the female body's text; most of the male characters are not capable of breaking through the binary system of language that identifies women as either virgins or whores. Men silence or decapitate (figuratively or literally) what they do not understand or what frightens them; *Titus Andronicus* is a story of decapitation. The dramatist exposes male characters who completely or partially misidentify the female body or are in the process of seeing how their constructs about women are the ruination of women, of men, and of relationships between the sexes. The title character and Bassianus, Lavinia's husband, are awakening to the deleterious effects of male containment of women; they are beginning to embrace *l'écriture féminine* or the voicing of the female body's text through their relationship with Lavinia. In psychological terms, each person never gets over the loss of the nurturing mother and the loss of the non-verbal language used between mother and child. Titus, in particular, evolves in the play, and the audience witnesses his struggle with the constructs of the nurturing versus the monstrous mother (Lavinia and Tamora, respectively). Lavinia's bodily text is the primary mover in the play, the discourse that changes the constructs that Titus and Bassianus believe in. Shakespeare fashions Lavinia to enlighten and elucidate. However, male characters in the play are totally blind and deaf to the female body's text and unfortunately do not grow at all from their encounters with Lavinia.

Lavinia represents the idea that female sexual power might be productive rather than destructive, that male constructs ordering the female body due to fear of the chaos of its text may be in error. Lavinia is raped, mutilated, constructed and re-constructed by male characters in a desperate attempt to stop the outpouring of her text, because her bodily text goes contrary to every construct of patriarchal society. Lavinia's personal traits are *entredeux*: her text exists in the gaps created by the male world of precepts and language. Therefore, the characters in the play do not want to embrace Lavinia's text: she is a woman who is sexual but not dangerous, who is powerful but also nurturing, who is tempting and also innocent. Her text cannot be true because if it is, then the binary system that constructs women as either virtuous or contaminated is a lie and must be completely re-named and re-ordered. Therefore, the male characters in the play must contain and edit Lavinia's text, must turn her physically into the monstrous woman, must eliminate her influence, must misread her text.

Societal constructs about women move women and men away from the mother tongue, the original force of expression learned from bonding with the mother before the child learns verbal language. The male dramatist must demonstrate his facility to connect with the mother tongue to disgorge, to translate the female characters' bodily text into writing. Shakespeare designs his plays as the site of maternal absence, which is why paternal authority reigns. The law and language of male society takes over the function of the mother of ordering or creating the world. Then, man no longer has need of the maternal body, no longer has a use for the archaic mother tongue (Cixous, "Laugh" 885). The issue that Shakespeare illustrates in his dramas is that even though the male characters figuratively decapitate the female body and try to smother its text, feminine text transcends masculine attempts to extinguish it. In *Titus Andronicus*, as in all of Shakespeare's tragedies, the dramatist embraces the chaos of the female body's text by outpouring loss that culminates in the last act of the drama.

Plot Summary

Titus Andronicus returns home to Rome victorious in battle in the Gothic wars. He brings with him Tamora, Queen of the Goths, and her three sons as the spoils of war. Because he has lost twenty-one sons in the war, he demands the death of her eldest son to avenge his losses, and although the queen pleads for her son's life, he is executed. Titus Andronicus is offered the Roman crown, but he upholds the claim of the late Emperor's son, Saturninus, to be the next in line for the throne. Saturninus and his brother Bassianus are in conflict over who is to become the next Emperor of Rome. With Titus Andronicus's help, Saturninus takes the throne and is offered the hand of Lavinia, Titus Andronicus's daughter, in marriage, even though she and Bassianus are involved in a secret love affair. Her brothers and Bassianus abduct her, and Bassianus and Lavinia are secretly married. Saturninus takes Tamora's hand in marriage in place of Lavinia. Tamora secretly vows to destroy Titus Andronicus and his whole family to avenge the death of her eldest son. Aaron, Tamora's lover, aids her sons, Chiron and Demetrius, in their plot to rape Lavinia. To assure that Chiron and Demetrius are not accused of attacking Lavinia, her tongue is cut out and her hands cut off. During the royal hunt, Bassianus and Lavinia stumble upon the love affair and secret meeting of Aaron and Tamora. Tamora calls upon her sons to assist her in keeping Bassianus and Lavinia quiet, and Chiron and

Demetrius murder Bassianus and attack Lavinia in the manner that they had planned. Aaron entices two of Titus Andronicus's sons to the scene and plants a bag of gold nearby. Aaron intends to implicate Andronicus's sons in the murder of Bassianus. Aaron arranges for Saturninus to show up at an appropriate moment, and Saturninus accuses Titus Andronicus's sons of the execution of his brother. Before Titus Andronicus's sons are executed for the murder of Bassianus, Aaron sends word that the Emperor will spare them if Lucius, one of the Andronici family, or Marcus, Andronicus's brother, will cut off a hand and send it to the Emperor as a token of good faith. Aaron manipulates Titus Andronicus into cutting off and sending his own hand to spare his son and brother as well as his two sons who are in custody awaiting execution. Later, Aaron viciously returns the hand and the severed heads of the accused sons to Titus Andronicus. Lucius is banished by the Emperor and raises an army among the Goths. Lavinia manages to communicate by manipulating a staff and drawing in the sand the names of her attackers. Titus pretends to be mad and plots his revenge on Tamora, Aaron, and Saturninus. Tamora gives birth to Aaron's child and Aaron takes possession of the boy. Aaron substitutes a white baby for the baby Tamora gave birth to, so that she can present the baby to the Emperor as his son. When fleeing from Rome with his child, Aaron is captured by Lucius and his army and tortured and maliciously admits to all of his heinous deeds before he dies. Titus Andronicus overpowers Tamora's sons, cuts their throats, and bakes them into a pie that at the Emperor's feast will be fed to Tamora and the Emperor. At the feast, Lavinia, who has been part of the revenge plot, appears dressed as a bride and Titus Andronicus kills her to put an end to her shame. He also kills Tamora to avenge the wrongs she has committed against his family. Saturninus defends his queen by killing Titus Andronicus, and Lucius slays Saturninus. Lucius explains the entire saga to the Roman people who declare him Emperor of Rome.

2. *Lavinia in Shakespeare's* Titus Andronicus

Figurative Decapitation

> Silence is the mark of hysteria. The great hysterics have lost speech,
> they are aphonic, and at times have lost more than speech: they are
> pushed to the point of choking, nothing gets through. They are
> decapitated, their tongues are cut off and what talks isn't heard
> because it's the body that talks, and man doesn't hear the body. In
> the end the woman pushed to hysteria is the woman who disturbs
> and is nothing but disturbance. (Cixous, "Castration" 171)

Lavinia is the perfect example of the "hysteric," figuratively
decapitated by the male characters in *Titus Andronicus*. Her voice and
sexuality are manipulated by the male figures in the play, and after her
rape and mutilation, she is "pushed to the point of choking" as she
tries to communicate her rapists' names to her family. For those who
view her plight, she is a disturbing presence in the drama. Most of the
male characters misread the disruptive female body's text;
misidentifying Lavinia's bodily text suppresses it.

Lavinia is figuratively decapitated by all the male characters in the
play, and Tamora also enables the suppression of Lavinia. Saturninus
uses Lavinia as a bargaining chip; his offer of marriage to her is made
as repayment for Titus' political support and as a manifestation of the
Emperor's desire "to advance / [Titus'] name and honorable family"
(1.1.238-39).[4] Lavinia's body will be the vessel that will house
Saturninus's progeny, the heirs to the throne. She is totally at the
mercy of male bonding; possession of her and of her sexuality is being
bartered for. Male possession of Lavinia is a part of her decapitation:
Bassianus claims to have prior possession of Lavinia when he states,
"Lord Titus, by your leave, this maid is mine" (1.1.276). A physical
fight breaks out over ownership of her, and Bassianus and Marcus
kidnap Lavinia. Bassianus explains that Lavinia has been "surprised [.
. .] by him that justly may / Bear his betroth'd from all the world
away" (1.1.285-86). However, Bassianus intimates that Lavinia is not

---

[4] All quotations from Shakespeare's texts are from *The Riverside Shakespeare*.

really "surprised" by his actions at all and that their mutuality of desire has separated them from the rest of the world of men and their misunderstanding of female *jouissance*. When Marcus, Bassianus, and Lavinia return to court later in the scene, Bassianus and Lavinia have married. Saturninus sarcastically concedes his claim on Lavinia stating, "So, Bassianus, you have play'd your prize. / God give you joy, sir, of your gallant bride!" (1.1.399-400).

Not only is Lavinia, but the female characters are collectively decapitated. Lavinia and Tamora are interchangeable commodities to Saturninus, which emphasizes their lack of individual worth and the devaluation of women in general. He offers one and then the other the position of Empress. First he approaches Titus:

> Titus Andronicus, for thy favors done
> To us in our election this day,
> I give thee thanks in part of thy deserts,
> And will with deeds requite thy gentleness;
> And for an onset, Titus, to advance
> Thy name and honorable family,
> Lavinia will I make my emperess,
> Rome's royal mistress, mistress of my heart,
> And in the sacred [Pantheon] her espouse.
> Tell me, Andronicus, doth this motion please thee?
>
> (1.1.234-43)

Saturninus sees his betrothal to Lavinia as an advancement for himself and for Titus within patriarchal society; Saturninus has no concern for her desires and only pays lip service to his attachment to her. Bassianus is the brother who truly sees Lavinia as the "mistress of [his] heart," because Bassianus is being changed by the power of her text, by her disgorgement. Saturninus's words of betrothal to Tamora are just as decapitating as his lack of understanding of Lavinia:

> And therefore, lovely Tamora, Queen of Goths,

That like the stately [Phoebe] 'mongst her nymphs
Dost overshine the gallant'st dames of Rome,
If thou be pleas'd with this my sudden choice,
Behold, I choose thee, Tamora, for my bride,
And will create thee Emperess of Rome. (1.1.314-20).

Although Saturninus addresses Tamora rather than her male family members for her hand as he does when he proposes to Lavinia, his words are no less denigrating. He concentrates on praising Tamora's beauty, objectifying her, as well as emphasizing his empowerment, revealing Saturninus's belief that he "chooses" and that he "creates" and re-creates the women within his sphere of influence. In this way, Saturninus attempts to usurp the power of creation from the archaic mother.

When he takes Tamora for his wife in 1.1, she says she will "a handmaid be to his desires" (331). The expressions "handmaid" and giving one's "hand in marriage" signify the contrasting relationships between the two women and Saturninus. Tamora uses the term "handmaid" to flatter Saturninus, but she has no intention of serving him. Lavinia is the character who is a handmaid to desire; she is not only the figure of the nurturing maternal body in the drama but Lavinia is a handmaid to the *jouissance* or outpouring of feelings concerning her oppressors and repressive constructs. She assists her family in their revenge plot against Tamora and her sons, and she helps Bassianus and Titus to a greater understanding of the female body's text.

The fact that Tamora and Lavinia are interchangeable as marriage partners for Saturninus is re-emphasized later in the play where Tamora and Lavinia are interchangeable to Demetrius and Chiron, as Coppelia Kahn argues (74). Demetrius and Chiron view these two women as representations of the devouring mother that Tamora's sons want to destroy. Because the two female characters in the play are set up as rivals for the hand of Saturninus from the outset of the play, the collective body of women is decapitated or split apart as well; Lavinia and Tamora are not positioned in the play to bond. Women in a male-governed society are put in a position where they must compete for the attentions of men who will be their protectors and providers; this condition alienates women from each other and is another form of decapitation. It is no wonder, therefore, that Tamora turns a deaf ear to Lavinia's pleas for death rather than rape by Tamora's sons; Tamora rebuffs Lavinia: "What beg'st thou then? Fond woman, let / me go" (2.3.172-73). Tamora enables the silencing of Lavinia by the male characters in the play.

Demetrius and Chiron have been witness to how Lavinia and Tamora are passed from one man to the next, but at the same time, Tamora's sons have seen their mother wield power politically and sexually over the other male characters in the play. For example, Tamora toys with Titus; she is disguised as "Revenge" in 5.2:

> Come down and welcome me to this world's light;
> Confer with me of murder and of death.
> There's not a hollow cave or lurking-place,
> No vast obscurity or misty vale,
> Where bloody murther or detested rape
> Can couch for fear, but I will find them out. (5.2.33-38)

Tamora represents the monstrous woman as she embodies "Revenge." She uses sexual wiles to manipulate Saturninus: "Then at my suit look graciously on him [Titus]; / Lose not so noble a friend on vain suppose, / Nor with sour looks afflict his gentle heart. / My lord, be rul'd by me, be won at last" (1.1.439-42). Her approach is no different with her lover, Aaron: "We may, each wreathed in the other's arms / (Our pastimes done), possess a golden slumber, / While hounds and horns and sweet melodious birds / Be unto us as is a nurse's song / Of lullaby to bring her babe asleep" (2.3.25-29). Here, Tamora links mothering to the hunt and to sexuality. In fact, it is her monstrous sexuality that is the catalyst for the rape and mutilation of Lavinia by

Demetrius and Chiron. This is of importance since Tamora's sons see that Lavinia and Tamora are viewed by Saturninus as interchangeable commodities. Demetrius's attitudes are clearly revealed when he states that women exist solely so that they may be woo'd, won, and taken from their husbands (2.1.82-89). Aaron and Tamora encourage her sons to avenge themselves on Lavinia: "Come, come, our empress, with her sacred wit, / To villainy and vengeance consecrate, / Will we acquaint withal what we intend" (2.1.120-22). Aaron feels certain that Tamora will sanction the violent sacrifice of Lavinia.

Tamora uses Lavinia's body as a toy as well, one to amuse her sons for a time, to occupy Demetrius and Chiron. Tamora tells Lavinia that she will not kill her because "So should I rob my sweet sons of their fee. / No, let them satisfice their lust on thee" (2.3.179-80). The subtext here is that Tamora wishes her sons to relieve their anxieties on Lavinia rather than on their mother; therefore, the rape of Lavinia's power will stand in for the annihilation of the mother. After all, Lavinia is newly married to Bassianus and could bear offspring, like Tamora has. Demetrius and Chiron have experienced the horror of living firsthand, as prisoners in the war between the Romans and Goths, and through the death of their brother, Alarbus, who, as a human sacrifice, was executed in 1.1, to atone for the loss of Titus's sons in the war with the Goths. Tamora brings Aaron's child into this world in 4.2, and Demetrius wants to kill the child (85-86). One purpose of killing the baby is so the child will not have to bear the burden of life's miseries that Demetrius has experienced. Chiron states, "I blush to think upon this ignominy" (4.2.115), and he is not only referring to the ruin of his mother in Saturninus's eyes. He also is speaking to the "ignominy" of being born.

The "abject" is Julia Kristeva's term for the chaos, black hole, or devouring abyss caused by the female body and its power over life and death that men fear (64). One manifestation of Kristeva's theory of the "abject" is the monstrous mother and the separation of self from maternal authority that Tamora embodies in the play (54). Lavinia's ability to become the nurturing mother is literally cut away from her by Demetrius and Chiron. They are attempting to eradicate the devouring maternal body. Shakespeare's Lavinia is set up as a contrasting figure to Tamora; Lavinia is the possibility of the nurturing mother that deconstructs the construct of the castrating mother. Tamora's sons fear maternal potential due to first-hand experience with their own mother.

The rape and mutilation of Lavinia is a transference or projection of Tamora's sons' fears. Since they feel impotent to desecrate their own mother, Demetrius and Chiron use Lavinia as a substitute for Tamora to purge their Freudian anxieties through ritual sacrifice to reorder their universe (Lincoln 13). Demetrius and Chiron are unchanged by their experience with Lavinia. They reveal in 4.2, that they define love and lust as synonymous (41-43). They believe it is the duty of women to "serve" (4.2.41) male desire; it is male prerogative to manipulate and use women. The female tongue is viewed as a castrating weapon, as Sheila Delaney argues (97). Aaron, Demetrius, and Chiron all indicate a desire to control Tamora and her speech; in their fantasy, she approves of their misuse of women and says "Amen" (4.2.44), sanctifying their oppression and brutality. They are mocking the entity that they fear, the maternal body giving birth: Demetrius sarcastically utters, "Come let us go and pray to all the gods / for our beloved mother in her pains" (4.2.46). The pain of women's subjugation and the pain of childbirth are connected here; women give life to the men who later oppress them.

Therefore, at the play's outset, Lavinia becomes the object of Demetrius and Chiron's oppression and displaced sexual desire. They also see the winning of Lavinia as a test of manhood and cunning; men avenge their family's dishonor and so Tamora's sons avenge their brother Alarbus's death at the hands of Titus (1.1.142) and win their mother's approval. After the rape and mutilation of Lavinia, Demetrius and Chiron feel assured that their identities as rapists will never be revealed.

Demetrius mocks Lavinia by saying, "So now go tell, and if thy tongue can speak, / Who 'twas that cut thy tongue and ravish'd thee" (2.4.1-2), and Chiron taunts, "Write down thy mind, betray thy meaning so, / And if thy stumps will let thee play the scribe" (2.4.3-4). The meaning of their gang rape, their decapitation of Lavinia, is inscribed indelibly upon her body, or so they think.

Demetrius's claim that he will "thrust those reproachful speeches down [Chiron's] throat, / That he hath breath'd in my dishonor here" (2.1.55) could also be applied to Demetrius's disfigurement of Lavinia later in 2.3. His fear of feminine text causes him to thrust the female body's text figuratively back down her throat, to suffocate that discourse, through rape and mutilation, and to replace her text with his own discourse of containment. Demetrius and Chiron represent patriarchal constructs about manhood and the control of femininity in their society: their discourse is loud and noisy but without substance. This is apparent where Chiron accuses Demetrius of being all talk and no action: "foul-spoken [. . .] thunder'st with thy tongue" (2.1.58). In addition, the court, bereft of the true mother tongue, echoes with noise, the sounds of the hunt in 2.2. The voice of the female body's text is silenced.

Demetrius calls Lavinia a "doe" that they will steal from her keeper, Bassianus (2.1.93-94); Aaron and Demetrius name Lavinia "a dainty doe" (2.1.117 and 2.2.26) and Aaron proclaims that "a solemn hunting is in hand" (2.1.112). Lavinia has been decapitated: she is not a woman but an animal to be hunted. Women who live under male supremacy have a perpetual wound, the construct that female sexuality is connected to animal lust. Even Lavinia's uncle, Marcus, describes her as an animal, "straying in the park, / Seeking to hide herself, as doth the deer / That hath receiv'd some un-recuring wound" (3.1.88-90). Rapists think that female eyes speak with sexuality, that the eyes say "yes" while the tongue says "no." Eyes speak the message of animality, but speech makes the person unique, not one of many. Male composite figures (part animal, part human) are heroes in Greek mythology, but female composite figures are monsters and sexual animals, according to Harold Eilberg-Schwartz and Wendy Doniger (28). In Julie Taymor's film version of *Titus Andronicus*, Lavinia is costumed in the rape scene wearing the head of a doe on a woman's body.[5] Since the female head is cut off, the composite figure consists of a bestial mind and body.

Aaron suggests that Demetrius and Chiron hunt Lavinia "and strike her home by force, if not by words" (2.1.117-18). If Demetrius and Chiron rape Lavinia, Aaron hopes that a power play will ensue between Tamora's sons and Titus's family. At the end of the play, Aaron tells the tale of his misdeeds and describes the mutilation of Lavinia as "trim sport" (5.1.96). The rape, like clitorectomies in certain societies, trims her of the "female propensity" to lascivious behavior. She is figuratively beheaded in the rape, freed of the "excess of adornment." The word 'trim' classifies Lavinia as a commodity, displayed as goods and suitably adjusted or put in good order. "Trimming" women keeps them in line; it is figurative decapitation. "Trimming" female sexuality was ingrained in Early Modern English society and appears in other works than *Titus Andronicus*; Jacobean tragedy is preoccupied with curtailing or redressing feminine sexuality.

Even Marcus, Lavinia's uncle, figuratively decapitates his niece. In 1.1, he welcomes and praises Titus and his kinsman's triumphant return home. Marcus believes that his nephews who have died in battle and will be interred in the family tomb "sleep in fame / [. . .] And triumph over chance in honor's bed" (1.1.173, 178). Chance or fortune is depicted as female in ancient cultures. Chance is violated here by death. The dead have "a safer triumph" (1.1.176) than the

---

[5] Julie Taymor's film version of *Titus Andronicus* greatly influenced my thinking concerning the depiction of Lavinia as the nurturing feminine body contrasted with Tamora as the monstrous mother. Lisa Starks's discussion of Lavinia and Tamora in her essay "*Powers of Horror* and Horrors of Power in Julie Taymor's *Titus*" assisted me in developing my own theories concerning Lavinia's decapitation and Shakespeare's textual disgorgement.

living. The tomb or womb of the maternal body has been transformed linguistically into the site of a rape. Marcus's statement foreshadows the literal rape of Lavinia in 2.3. The site of the tomb that Titus has venerated earlier in this scene is violated by masculine ideals just as Lavinia, whose virtue is honored by Titus, is raped by Demetrius and Chiron who enforce the constructs of men to order and contain women. Therefore, Marcus sees the tomb not as Titus does but as a site where "fame" and "honor," masculine constructs, can be forcibly inscribed.

It is denigrating to the female body as text that the men in *Titus Andronicus* try to inscribe meaning to the maternal body depicted as the Andronici tomb just as they try to force their own description on Lavinia's wounds. Marcus's belabored speech (2.4.11-57) attempts to contain the disorder of her violated bodily condition:

> O, that I knew thy heart, and knew the beast,
> That I might rail at him to ease my mind!
> Sorrow concealed, like an oven stopp'd,
> Doth burn the heart to cinders where it is.
> Fair Philomela, why, she but lost her tongue,
> And in a tedious sampler sew'd her mind;
> But, lovely niece, that mean is cut from thee.
> A craftier Tereus, cousin, hast thou met,
> And he that cut those pretty fingers off
> That could have better sew'd than Philomel. (2.4.34-43)

Marcus uses words to try to heal Lavinia; he tosses words at her as if the power of language alone will close her wounds, will re-construct the truth that he sees before him concerning the decapitating effects of patriarchal constructs. The length of his statement, like Montaigne's ironic testament to the power of bodily text, is in itself a testimony to the fact that Lavinia's bodily disorder cannot be controlled by language. Marcus tries to impose his own meaning on her deformed figure when he finds her shortly after the rape: "Shall I speak for thee?

Shall I say 'tis so?" (2.4.33). When presenting Lavinia to Titus after her rape, Marcus describes her mutilated form as loss and lack; Marcus speaks about her in past tense as if she is already dead: "This was thy daughter" (3.1.62). Lucius, like Marcus, sees Lavinia as voiceless, a blank page on which the men in his family should inscribe meaning, as Evelyn Gajowski observes (2). Lucius demands that Marcus speak for Lavinia: "O, say thou for her, who hath done this deed [the mutilation of Lavinia]?" (3.1.87). Lucius and Marcus are attempting to re-inscribe Lavinia's text and its connection to the mother tongue. Later in 3.1,

> there is, as Jonathan Bate says, an implied stage direction at this moment, for Marcus says to Lavinia: 'Alas, poor heart, that kiss is comfortless / As frozen water to a sarved snake' (251-52). Samuel Johnson introduced a direction for Lavinia to kiss Lucius, which subsequent editors changed to Lavinia kissing Titus. Bate, however acutely realized that Lavinia must here *kiss the heads of her brothers*: such a kiss earns Marcus's sad comment on its lack of consolation, but this comment shows, in turn, how easily Lavinia's signs are mis-read, or ignored. Her kissing of the heads intends not comfort, but expiation, a demonstration of the brothers' innocence that remains an uncertain fact in the minds of her uncle and father. (Hutson 50)

Thus, Lavinia's text once again is misread and disregarded.

In 4.1, the Andronici men think Lavinia's antics mean she is mad even though she is simply trying to communicate with them about her rape and mutilation. Lucius describes Lavinia's disruptive force when she chases him to point out Ovid's *Metamorphoses* containing the story of the raped Philomela as a communication by Lavinia concerning her attackers. Lavinia is this woman in *Titus Andronicus*; she is the embodiment of the nurturing female as "prey" to masculinity, Cixous's definition of the "hysteric" ("Castration" 168) in the drama.

After her rape and mutilation, Marcus and Lucius depict her behavior as hysterical, out of control. According to men, a woman like Lavinia who is attempting to speak must be hysterical or mad: "some fit or frenzy do possess her" (4.1.17) and the "extremity of griefs would make [even] men mad" (4.1.19).

Hysteria is constructed by the patriarchy of Early Modern England to be "a rising up of the womb out of its place" (Jardine 110), the woman behaving in a disorderly manner that men must contain. Marcus views Lavinia in the same manner that he defines Rome, as a figuratively decapitated female body that needs a head, male reason, to complete her: "Be *candidatus* then and put it on, / And help to set a head on headless Rome" (1.1.185-86). Marcus tells the "sons of Rome" (5.3.67) at the end of the play: "Let me teach you how to knit / [. . .] these broken limbs again into one body" (5.3.70-72). He blames Rome for doing "shameful execution on herself" (5.3.76). The female body, figured as Rome, is continuously being figuratively decapitated, blamed for her own destruction, and then reconstructed by the male characters in the play.

The ultimate symbol of Lavinia's decapitation is her rape and disfigurement. A woman who is raped is ruined in terms of marriageability in a patriarchal society. I agree with Kahn that Lavinia's exchange value is nullified by the rape, but I don't agree that her symbolic value is destroyed (49). Lavinia's bodily text has value even after her violation. The raped woman embodies the persona of the temptress and the site of sexual promiscuity; she is transformed into the body of the monstrous maternal body. Tamora superimposes Lavinia's chasteness in marriage, which Lavinia throws in her face right before the rape scene, with a woman's virginity. This gives Demetrius a pretext to gain figurative power over his mother by raping Lavinia: "This minion stood upon her chastity, / Upon her nuptial vow, her loyalty / [. . .] And shall she carry this unto her grave?" (2.3.124-27). The raped Lavinia is the woman whose sexuality, creativity, and birthing of children are ordered by the patriarchy.

To separate from the void of the monstrous mother which threatens their sense of individuated identity from women, Demetrius and Chiron not only rape but also mutilate Lavinia. Her mutilation is figuratively decapitating. Bassianus takes Lavinia's hand in marriage, and Demetrius and Chiron mock this ceremonial passage of women from the hands or possession of one man to another by cutting her hands off in 2.4. Demetrius and Chiron think the mutilation of Lavinia has dis-figured her so that she cannot identify her killers nor be handed off to anyone else within the masculine economy because she is socially and sexually soiled. Without hands, as Katherine Rowe points out, Lavinia has no connection between herself and the outside world; she is literally and figuratively cut off (70). The hand can represent a contract or consent (14, 24); Lavinia's hand is the contract with her husband dissolved by Demetrius and Chiron murdering Bassianus. Lavinia's hands also represent her rape, her lack of consent. According to Rowe, hands stand for "giving," as Lavinia does not give herself freely to her rapists, and for "taking," as Lavinia's chastity and agency are taken from her by her assailants (10).

The head represents thought or intent and the hand is action and personal power; the head regulates and restrains the hand. So, Lavinia's hands represent female containment in the patriarchy, the role of woman that must be ordered and constructed by male language. Lavinia's hands become absent signifiers of the collective signifying body; her hands reveal the commodification of women in the marriage market. Titus becomes disconnected from the male collective body when he agrees to give his hand away to ransom his sons Quintus and Martius in 3.1. Without hands, Lavinia and Titus are severed from the dominating grip of judgment and acquisition in male-governed society and are free to return through death to the site of the maternal womb/tomb, as Rowe explains (80). The high body count in this play does not reflect the voracious maternal body but instead is Shakespeare's illustration of the destructive force of dogma on the individual and on society, but especially as dogma applies to women, embodied in Lavinia's figurative decapitation.

Enforcing chastity and virginity in Early Modern England was figurative rape, one form of silencing (Loughlin 86). The mutilation of Lavinia's mouth is a silencing, a figurative and literal sexual violation of her. By cutting her tongue away, her rapists ironically believe they have restored order to sexual disorder. The maiming and disfiguring of the female mouth in the Early Modern period, as Lynda Boose illustrates, was connected to the disorder created by female voice and sexuality (258). An example of the disorder of female license to speak occurs earlier in the drama when Lavinia speaks in opposition to the Emperor's assertion that the call to the hunt has sounded "somewhat too early for new-married ladies" (2.2.15). With an absent tongue, the power of Lavinia's sexuality and verbal license has been eliminated; this woman can no longer usurp male dominion over sexuality and language.

The term "mother tongue" is a misnomer since the disgorgement of text is the only true mother tongue. Demetrius and Chiron attempt to extract the mother tongue from Lavinia, a substitute for Tamora, who gave them access to the true mother tongue, the disgorgement of the body as text at birth; this is the tongue that phallocentrism destroys through its containment of women. Men want to eliminate any connection for women or for men with the original mother tongue, the body as text, because that text displaces patriarchal text or the primacy of the phallus. Being subsumed back into the mother means the loss of everything that patriarchal culture has established: the supremacy of man over woman. The original mother tongue blurs the boundaries between bodies. Fear of the blurring between bodies, being sucked back into mother, causes Demetrius and Chiron to rape and mutilate.

The forest where Lavinia is raped and disfigured is paralleled with her; the woods are figured as a place without language, without a tongue, a place of figurative decapitation: "the woods are ruthless, dreadful, deaf and dull" (2.1.128). Instead, the woods are the site of the archaic mother and her tongue. They are also contrasted with the palace, the seat of male discourse: "The palace full of tongues, of eyes, and ears" (2.1.127). The palace is described as a head, and the forest is the female body; the palace possesses many body parts but not the text of the female body. Aaron describes the forest as "wide and spacious, / And many unfrequented plots there are" (2.1.114-15), the very description of the pit in 2.4, that is the representation of the womb of the consuming maternal body. Men of the court have abandoned the "unfrequented plots" that comprise the maternal body. Male constructs must be forced upon the mother tongue, "there [in the woods] speak and strike, brave boys" (2.1.129), because the primeval maternal body cannot hear the authoritative commands of the patriarchy. Male language is unintelligible to this site.

Saturninus explains the Early Modern male viewpoint of women when he says that it was right of Virginius to slay his daughter after she had been "enforc'd, stain'd, and deflow'r'd" (5.3.38) "because the girl should not survive her shame, / And by her presence still renew his sorrows" (5.3.41-42). This is not the reason that Titus slays Lavinia; Titus only asks this question of Saturninus to prove how little the Emperor understands the female body's text. Lavinia has indeed survived, is not shamed, and her presence has given a strength to her kinsman. Titus is "woeful" like Virginius but not for the same reason. The figurative decapitation of women is an "outrage" (5.3.52).

The very things that are done to Lavinia by the patriarchy – mutilation that creates incoherence and incapacity – is actually the property and composition of these men and not of Lavinia or of other women; these things are projected on to women. Lavinia's rapists intend the mutilation of her mouth to stand as a signifier of her rape; therefore, her bodily text reflects her disgrace. Lawrence Danson sees Lavinia as a representative of humanity's pain, the need to be understood (1). Often, her bodily text has been consumed into mankind or humanity's meaning in past criticism. Men in a patriarchy do to women what they fear women will do to them: men consume women into the text of men. However, Lavinia's disgorgement is a departure; Shakespeare's drama reveals the text of Lavinia to illuminate the female condition, specifically the situation of women of his time period.

Lavinia is created to be a disgorgement that subverts Early Modern English constructs. Therefore, her body transfigures her decapitation; her form disappears behind the weight of the context, the multitude of meanings the mutilated female body represents. Lavinia's continued appearance in society after she has been permanently soiled and tossed aside empowers the purity of her character and deconstructs male tenets concerning women as property and female propriety. Her scars are voices; they bear witness to the degradation of women in ancient society and in Early Modern society. Shakespeare turns Lavinia's figurative decapitation into a disgorgement. What does her despoiled body as text "say"?

Disgorgement

> The movement of the [female] text doesn't trace a straight line [. . .]
> I see it as an outpouring [. . .] as vomiting, as 'throwing up,'
> 'disgorging.' (Cixous, "Castration" 176)

Shakespeare creates an outpouring or disgorgement of text by releasing Lavinia's "voice" from containment. Although her mutilation disempowers her physically, the depth of metaphor attached to her after the rape, a text that "doesn't trace a straight line," becomes a textual disgorgement and "strikes [male sovereignity] home by force" (2.1.118 *Titus Andronicus*), undermining Aaron's statement with the significance of her presence. She becomes a power that cannot be extinguished.

As part of her disgorgement, Lavinia always inhabits the *entredeux* space in the play: between Titus and Saturninus, Saturninus and

Tamora, Saturninus and Bassianus, and between Chiron and Demetrius. Although Saturninus announces that he will make her his empress, it is apparent that he sees Lavinia's body as a trophy that he has been awarded by Titus. Women are handed from man to man through the marriage ceremony in patrilineal societies. Saturninus asks for Lavinia's hand in marriage, but Tamora has already caught his eye. Saturninus remarks, in an aside, when he first sees Tamora: "A goodly lady, trust me, of the hue / That I would choose were I to choose anew" (1.1.261-62). Lavinia's betrothal to Saturninus places her in a position between Tamora and her hopes to position herself in Saturninus's court as empress. Saturninus and Bassianus both vie for the hand of Lavinia. Saturninus tells his brother, Bassianus, that he will "repent this rape" (1.1.404), the stealing of Lavinia as Saturninus's bride. Saturninus feels that his brother has usurped the emperor's rightful position as Lavinia's husband. Demetrius and Chiron compete for Lavinia's attentions; she is a prize to be won to prove their virility and cunning to Tamora:

> Chiron: I care not, I, knew she and all the world,
> I love Lavinia more than all the world.
> Demetrius: Youngling, learn thou to make some meaner
>   choice,
> Lavinia is thine elder brother's hope. (2.1.71-74)

Lavinia's disgorgement is revealed in the subversion of the binary system of language and its constructs. In other words, she does not fit neatly within the story of the play; ultimately, she does not belong to any of the male characters in the drama.

Lavinia's generosity of spirit is also part of her outpouring of text. She is the dutiful daughter who celebrates her father's fame and rise in status: "My noble lord and father, live in fame!" (1.1.158). "O bless me here with thy victorious hand, / Whose fortune Rome's best citizens applaud" (1.1.163-64). Lavinia is approving (1.1.270-71) towards the compassionate, "princely usage" (1.1.266) of Tamora, their prisoner of war. Lavinia expresses the qualities of selfless obedience to her father and to her sovereign. She fulfills her father's prophesy in 1.1 to "live [. . .] for virtue's praise" (167-68). The male characters attempt to trivialize Lavinia's text, but her words are sometimes bold and sarcastic; for example, she reproaches Saturninus when he asks her if she is displeased by his words to Tamora: "Not I, my lord; sith true nobility / Warrants these words in princely courtesy" (1.1.271-72). Lavinia refers to "true nobility," the bodily text that she represents, and how her "true nobility" transforms the patronizing manners and licentious thoughts, the text of the patriarchy, into "courtesy" or generosity, authorizing or warranting true words of comfort to all women. Lavinia's words overthrow Saturninus's meaning and also his attempt to manage her. She displaces the male economy of exchange with the nurturing female economy of courtesy that consists of allowance, cooperation, respect, and indulgence.

The effect of her text is most prominently depicted in her relationships with her lover and with her father. Although men would be schooled in a language and law that objectifies and oppresses women, Shakespeare imbues some of his male characters with an ability to embrace a bisexual discourse, both the masculine and feminine aspects of language. Male language deals with constructs of patriarchy, such as honor, fame, order and hierarchy, whereas female discourse reflects qualities inscribed upon it by male society, such as obedience, humility and graciousness, as well as characteristics of the maternal body. Shakespeare illustrates how Lavinia is able to manifest and at the same time manipulate the characteristics of "female discourse" to her advantage. Rome is depicted in sections of the drama as a woman, and "Rome's richest ornament" (1.1.52) would be her virginity or virtue, the quality that Lavinia embodies. Although Bassianus's language sometimes objectifies Lavinia's sexuality, as in the description just quoted, Bassianus also uses words that are soft and yielding about her, such as "and her to whom my thoughts are humbled all, / Gracious Lavinia" (1.1.51-52). Bassianus admits that his "thoughts," the constructs of male society, are all humbled to the goodness of Lavinia, whose text throughout the play is all about the nurturing woman.

Titus, like Bassianus, is crafted by Shakespeare as a man who is beginning to embrace the female body's text. This is most evident in his description of the Andronici family tomb in 1.1, that holds the bodies of many of Titus's sons killed in the war with the Goths. Lucius, Titus's son, views the tomb as an "earthly prison of their bones," (1.1.99) a site of "shadows" (1.1.100) and "disturbance" (1.1.101), much in the way that Kristeva describes the "abject" and its connection to the monstrous mother. Lucius is frightened by the tomb and envisions this space as a dreaded place producing demons; he wants to produce a sacrifice of the hewed limbs of his enemy to appease the power of the tomb. It is most striking that Titus, instead of railing in anger or fear at the tomb as his son does, speaks words that are respectful and reverent:

> Make way to lay them by their bretheren [. . .]
> There greet in silence, as the dead are wont,
> And sleep in peace, slain in your country's wars!
> O sacred receptacle of my joys,
> Sweet cell of virtue and nobility [. . .]" (1.1.89-93)

It is clear from this passage that family is precious to Titus just as it is to Bassianus; Bassianus tells Marcus that he "love[s] and honor[s] thee and thine" (1.1.49), the family of Lavinia, the woman he loves. In addition, this is the only scene in the play in which a man (Titus) faces a bleeding pit, in this case the tomb holding the wounded dead bodies of his sons, with grace and acceptance rather than with horror and loathing. The Andronici tomb in 1.1, and 5.1 is a part of the disgorgement that Shakespeare creates.

The dead are sleeping in peace, removed from the chaos of society's attempts to order what cannot be ordered, the disruptive force of life and its connection to the archaic mother. Titus explains this theme in act 1: "In peace and honor rest you here, my sons, / Rome's readiest champions, repose you here in rest, / Secure from worldly chances and mishaps! / Here lurks no treason, here no envy swells [. . .]" (1.150-53). These dead are "secure from worldly chances" in a "sacred receptacle" or "sweet cell" (1.1.91-93). One of his meanings is that the tomb is revered and noble because his valiant sons reside there and define the nature of the site. However, lines 92, 93, and 152 in 1.1 can also be interpreted as Titus coming to peace with death even at the outset of the play, that the male fear of returning to the maternal body is unfounded. Titus speaks directly to the tomb, as if he is conversing or creating a dialogue with the image of the maternal body.

Later in 1.1, Titus professes to have "sumptuously re-edified" (351) the family tomb. He has not just rebuilt the tomb; he has restructured its meaning. Here Shakespeare addresses the issue of *differance*, the disparity between word and meaning. The tomb now instructs the mother tongue; it enlightens those "soldiers and Rome's servitors" (352) who are laid to rest there. Titus thinks he has restructured the tomb, but the tomb has actually rearranged Titus's thinking. He believes he is protecting the tomb from penetration by undeserving usurpers. He may be misguided about his "unworthy brother, and unworthy sons" (346) but not about the tomb's edifying powers. The Andronici monument is indeed "virtue's nest" (376). Mutius died in honor for Lavinia's or virtue's cause. Men may live in fame, but they die and are buried in the nest or site of virtue.

Titus sees himself as a gallant "soldier" (1.1.193) or champion of Rome, who is a "glorious" (1.1.187) female. He also depicts Rome as Lavinia's maternal guardian: "Kind Rome, that hast thus lovingly reserv'd / The cordial of mine age to glad my heart!" (1.1.165-66). Lavinia's embodiment of *l'écriture féminine* and her outpouring of feelings of devotion to her father affects the way he reads the female body. Titus depicts Rome as feminine, not as the site of masculine aggression. In like manner, Lavinia's love for Bassianus has influenced his figurative relationship with the female body and its text. He loves Lavinia as well and is beginning to turn his back on male dominion in favor of her; he believes that he is "possess'd of that is mine" (1.1.408). Bassianus does not say he owns Lavinia but that they possess each other. He sarcastically retorts that the "laws" of Rome as the true mother tongue will ultimately "determine all" (1.1.407). He explains that he owes his "duties" (1.1.414) to his vision of Rome as the nurturing female body. These statements foreshadow his own gruesome death at the hands of two representatives of the ancient law of men, Demetrius and Chiron (depicted as Rape and Murder in 5.2), and his return to mother earth in 2.3.

In 3.1, Marcus is afraid of the outpouring of Titus's passions that are not controlled by reason (218). However, Titus has touched the body of mother earth and is engulfed by it: "I am the sea / [. . .] I [am] the earth" (3.1.225-26). This connects Titus to Lavinia, and he is identifying with the feminine side of himself: "Then must my sea be moved with her sighs; / Then must my earth with her continual tears / Become a deluge" (3.1.228-29). He vomits her woes (3.1.231). Disgorgement is a vomiting of text. Lavinia's compassion for Titus changes him; she kisses him when the heads of her brothers, accused of murdering Bassianus, are returned to them (3.1.249). Her love helps her father to accurately read the text of the female body.

Lavinia continues to be loving towards young Lucius even after her rape and mutilation; she plays with him and they look at books together (4.1). Young Lucius admits that Lavinia "loves me as dear as e'er my mother did" (4.1.23), which connects Lavinia to the comforting maternal body. Lavinia read to Lucius before her attack just as a supportive mother would; Titus indicates that "Cornelia never with more care / Read to her sons than she [Lavinia] that read to thee [Lucius]" (4.1.12-13). The text Lavinia searches for is Ovid's *Metamorphoses* with its tale of the rape of Philomel; young Lucius explains that his mother gave him the book (4.1.42), a text that reveals the bodily discourse of the abuse of women by men. Marcus explains Lavinia's interest in the book by stating that "for love of her that's gone [Lucius's mother], / Perhaps, she [Lavinia] cull'd [the book] from among the rest" (4.1.43-44). In other words, for love of the mother, Lavinia attempts to communicate her text to her family. Like young Lucius, she is motherless in the drama. Maternal absence in her case functions in this drama to isolate and spotlight her, to compare her isolation and lack of comforting mother to the male fear of the dreadful mother and the lack of a nurturing mother in the play. If Shakespeare is right that the "hand [is] the agent of the heart" (*Two Gentleman of Verona* 1.3.46), then Lavinia's disembodied hands symbolize the outpouring of expression and feelings of the nurturing female. The disembodied hands of Lavinia speak in a way that her hands could not if she wrote out or if she signed her text, as Rowe indicates (12).

Subversion of Language

> A feminine text cannot fail to be more than subversive. It is volcanic [. . . it exists] to shatter the framework of institutions, to blow up the law, to break up the 'truth.' (Cixous, "Laugh" 888)

Lavinia's repeated presence in each scene of the play creates a textual subversion that shatters the "framework" of Roman and Gothic law as embodied by Saturninus and Tamora's family and breaks up the "truth" that her father has lived by. *Titus Andronicus* is about the perils of rhetoric, how instead of partnering the bodily text, it often stifles this text, especially the mother tongue and its disgorgement. Shakespeare creates a disgorgement of text through Lavinia's character that decapitates or deconstructs language. For example, her bodily presence on stage after her rape and mutilation in Titus Andronicus not only stands for the words 'rape,' 'mutilation,' 'decapitation,' 'victimization' but also for all of the things that these words imply about a woman encaged by Early Modern patriarchal beliefs. Shakespeare shows that Lavinia's dismembered figure is a disruption of hierarchy and a turbulence that destabilizes male systems including male language. The Early Modern English patriarchy, Boose explains, characterized Eve's seductive mouth as bringing disorder to the world (263); in *Titus Andronicus*, Lavinia's subversive verbal discourse in acts 1 and 2 and her vacant, mutilated mouth after act 2 bring disorder to male text. However, her empty mouth defines her as the disorder of the mother tongue, a text that subverts the masculine label of Eve's "evil" placed upon women in Early Modern England by demonstrating what figurative decapitation does to women.

Lavinia is denigrated before, during, and after the gang rape. Demetrius's attitude towards women is clearly deprecating with no regards for what women desire: "She is a woman, therefore may be woo'd, / She is a woman, therefore may be won, / She is Lavinia, therefore must be lov'd" (2.1.82-84). His discourse is meant to belittle and objectify women. After her mutilation in 2.3, Lavinia embodies the denigrated woman of Ovidian discourse, because she no longer possesses the parts of a woman that can be praised in poetic terms. However, her bodily text, her continued presence in the play, especially after her rape and mutilation, undermines Demetrius's attempt to diminish her meaning.

I concur with Heather James, who professes that the text describing Lavinia's mutilation is Ovidian as well as Petrarchan in tone (1). James indicates that Lavinia's rape is used by Shakespeare to "scrutinize the art of Petrarchan representation" and that Lavinia's character "becomes a palimpsest bearing the literary and ideological inscriptions of Virgil, Ovid, Petrarch and finally, Shakespeare" (47).

Frank Kermode's scathing criticism of James's use of academic vocabulary punctuates the very thing that Shakespeare examines through Lavinia's character – the subversion of stereotypical "male" texts. Kermode believes that Lavinia succumbs to the language of (male-dominated) US academia (9). However, he fails to take into account that some women in contemporary academia (as well as in Eden, ancient Judea, ancient Rome, and Early Modern England, as this book discusses) undermine discourse by embracing the language of the oppressor and then manipulating it. Shakespeare uses Lavinia to dismantle the power of stereotypically male discourses, texts like Ovid's and Virgil's. Therefore, her bodily text, her continued presence in the play, especially after her rape and mutilation, not only undermines Demetrius's attempt to diminish her meaning but deconstructs the binary opposition of Ovidian versus Petrarchan and Virgilian discourses. The text of Lavinia's character is at once all of these and none of these.

Her mutilation represents a mockery of the ideal woman, because body parts like women's hands were praised in Petrarchan discourse. Lavinia's body "queers" the Petrarchan blazon that anatomizes women. Taymor critiques the Petrarchan blazon by putting the ruined Lavinia on a pedestal in her film version of the play. Lavinia on the pedestal is not the ideal woman but the woman transformed into a monster by patriarchal containment. Taymor's depiction of Lavinia on the pedestal is supported by the behavior of the male characters in the play; Saturninus, Marcus, Aaron, Demetrius, and Chiron all view Lavinia as the spoils of war, a trophy to be displayed, in one sense or another. It is not Lavinia but the norms of the Early Modern patriarchy that are monstrous.

Physical unchastity in Early Modern England was considered the same as verbal license (Ferguson 242). Therefore, Lavinia's text also ridicules the patriarchy's construct that the ideal woman is silent, obedient, and chaste. Lavinia is silent; she has no tongue. Lavinia is obedient; she has no hands. Lavinia is chaste; she has been gang raped, an action that beheads or neuters her sexuality. Her lack, her missing tongue and hands, is her decapitation and is used to illustrate the futility of patriarchal ordering of female chaos that in reality, rather than creating containment, just perpetuates more disorder. Therefore, Lavinia's bodily "lack" is used by Shakespeare to critique male constructs; as Marcus points out, "what stern ungentle hands / Hath lopp'd and hew'd, and made thy body bare / Of her two branches" (2.4.16-18).

Tamora appears on the surface to have the body and face of the ideal woman, yet she is not cognizant of the text of the virtuous female body: "I know not what it means" (2.3.157). Lavinia entreats Tamora "to open [her] deaf ears," (2.3.160) to allow Lavinia to re-teach the mother tongue to her, but Tamora will not be reminded of the maternal body she has turned her back on. Lavinia's bodily text disables the binary system of coding or labeling women. The female characters in this play are created as stereotypes to deconstruct the binary system of language. In an aside as a response to Demetrius, young Lucius says in 4.2, "you are both decipher'd, that's the news" (8). Shakespeare creates Lavinia's bodily text to reverse and reveal meaning; it has transformed and decoded the text of Demetrius and Chiron for everyone to read. She has reduced her rapists to ciphers, non-entities which was exactly what they hoped to do to her and what male society tries to do to all women. Her bodily text has reduced the weight of male text.

It is important that the last words Lavinia utters are "Confusion fall [. . .]" (2.3.184). She summons the chaos of her father's revenge and that of the bodily text of the female hysteric in this scene. Her words come true in act 5, where the chaos of her own text causes the male characters that comprise her family in the play to bring about the ruination of her rapists, of their mother, of their mother's lover, and of the Emperor. The dramatist constructs female martyrdom in the play to place the woman completely outside the male symbolic, outside male jurisdiction as represented in language, in a place where true "female" discourse can originate as a disruption of the system. Lavinia's death is a sacrifice, a generation of the discourse of loss where the body is given up to attain a higher level of expression. Martyrdom composes a meaning that cannot be eclipsed by male discourse. Lavinia's death makes her body as "referent" disappear so that nothing but epitaph remains.

In the murder of Demetrius and Chiron, Titus stops their mouths (5.2.167) that cry in protest in a similar manner to the way her rapists prevent Lavinia's mouth from crying out by cutting out her tongue. Also, they are to "hear what fearful words" Titus utters (5.2.168), just as Lavinia was forced to hear Demetrius and Chiron's words during her attack. Titus intends to bake Demetrius and Chiron's heads, representing the heads of men of the patriarchy, the heads of reason, and feed them to Tamora, back into the body of the monstrous mother which is a text that men have created, effectively neutralizing male power over the perpetration of "Rape," "Murder" (5.2.45), and "Revenge" (5.2.3) against women and all mankind. By executing Demetrius and Chiron, Titus is effectively suffocating male language and destroying its constructs. In 5.3, Titus tells the court that Demetrius and Chiron's "mother daintily hath fed, / Eating the flesh that she herself hath bred" (5.3.61-62).

Titus does all of this to make a statement concerning the figurative decapitation of his daughter. He proposes that he was not the one who slayed Lavinia; it was actually Demetrius and Chiron (5.3.56). Titus is aware that if he kills Tamora, Saturninus or someone in the court will kill him, so he brings about his own death, or merging with the nurturing maternal body, through Tamora's murder. The deaths of Titus, Bassianus, and Lavinia are not described as idealistic romanticism. The deaths of these characters represent the dramatist's disgorgement, like birthing, a loss, a giving, that are not intended to be identified, manipulated, or reconsumed back into the structures and constructs of the hierarchy.

Jouissance **through Bisexual Discourse**

> This self-effacing, merger-type bisexuality [of text . . .] is each one's location in self of the presence [. . .] of both sexes, non-exclusion either of the difference or of one sex, and from this 'self-permission,' multiplication of the effects of the inscription of desire over all parts of [the] body. (Cixous, "Laugh" 884)

The author who disgorges is penetrated by the desire to express a merger of text, a bisexual discourse; the writer who disgorges deconstructs the gap in the binary system of language and fills this gap to overflowing. Shakespeare constructs Lavinia's gang rape so that it can be displaced by another kind of "penetration," the desire to express rather than repress. Lavinia deconstructs "the gap" in her attempts to communicate her rapists' names to her family and fills it in communication to overflowing (without the use of tongue or hands) by using her body as a text of her own personal *jouissance*. Lavinia's text is her figurative baby, the one she did not get an opportunity to bear.

Lavinia collaborates in Titus' revenge plot against her rapists, collecting the blood of the murdered Demetrius and Chiron in a basin; Titus explains that his "one hand yet is left to cut your throats, / While that Lavinia 'tween her stumps doth hold / The basin that receives your guilty blood" (5.2.203). The blood of her rapists is the ink Lavinia uses to assert her text in this scene. Their blood fills her basin, representing her violated womb; the visual image of her collecting the blood creates a statement about her mutilated condition, her desecrated womb that will never be filled with human life but that is now filled with the life of her oppressors, the body as text. The blood of her attackers inseminates a female narrative about the monstrosity of the violation of women by male-governed society and creates a figurative coitus through a joining of male and female discourses. "As Lavinia's body inspires Titus's literary revenge, so it serves as the text to reveal, authorize, and complete it" (James 78). Titus declaims the actions of men towards nature, depicted as female in the play: "O had we never, never hunted there!" (4.1.56) and elicits the female body's text: "Give signs, sweet girl" (4.1.61). Lavinia writes her rapists' names using Marcus's staff. I disagree with Kahn that writing in Latin reinscribes her existence with the text "of her cultural dominators" (62) and obscures the context her mutilated body represents. Instead of depending on the medium of "the feminine art of textiles" to tell her story like the raped Philomel, Lavinia translates the body's text into writing to explain her situation. Following Marcus's example of writing with the staff in the sand, Lavinia uses the Latin word *stuprum* as the means to translate the body's text into a language the male characters who comprise her family can understand (4.1.78).

For Clark Hulse and Douglas Green, Lavinia's use of the stick in her mouth to write the names of her rapists is a fellatio-like action that reenacts her rape, enabling her own oppression (116, 325). Caterina Romeo's interpretation of Lavinia's action is similar, stating that because Lavinia is "trapped in the male discourse, the only way in which she is allowed to express herself is by symbolically enacting fellatio" (88). I totally disagree with this reading of Lavinia's body. Indeed, Lavinia's appearance with the staff in her mouth parallels the humiliation of female "scolds" in Early Modern England who were bridled in iron masks that had long tongues and put on display in the marketplace (Boose 267). The tongue of the bridle looks like a phallus stopping up the mouth of the woman. Bridling was intended to stop the voice of a woman through a rape of the mouth. However, Lavinia's fellatio, using the staff as a pen/penis to inscribe her meaning in the dust, is a "queering" of the sexual practice of fellatio, a subversion of male dominance over language used to enunciate her rapists' identities. Also, Shakespeare's text that he invents for Lavinia's disgorgement is doubly "queered" since there is a *jouissance* of merged texts as Shakespeare joins his text with Ovid's text of Philomela in *Metamorphoses*. However, Shakespeare's text is more of a disgorgement than Ovid's, as Albert H. Tricomi points out, because by "having Lavinia scrawl out the names of her ravishers by holding a pole between her stumps and grasping the pole's end inside her mouth [. . .] Lavinia's lips do speak; her handless hands, indeed, do write" (233). In this way, her body is her voice and Shakespeare's voice as well; her body takes the place of her mutilated mouth that cannot speak and her deformed arms that cannot write. The use of her body, rather than her hands or tongue, to write or speak is a creation of bisexual discourse, using the staff as a phallic instrument. The female body is not only the force behind the writing implement (the staff as phallus) but also the text itself.

The male characters in *Titus Andronicus* are active, speaking, and commanding. The blank page women are made into is figuratively raped by the pen(is) (Gubar 295). Lavinia's bodily text changes this process into a discourse between or an intercourse of male and female by taking the phallus/pole in her mouth. This action is significant and signifying, appropriating male symbols of signification, of authority, the phallus and Latin, to translate the body's text for her family. Marcus is unsettled by and resistant to Lavinia's action of writing with the staff even though he instructed her to do it; he finds the figurative birth of bodily text created by the joining of the female body with the staff as the phallic pen, using writing as a medium of translation by women of the female body's text, to "stir a mutiny in mildest thoughts" (4.1.85), something that would "arm the minds of infants" (4.1.86). To Marcus, Lavinia with the staff in her mouth appears to be the figure of what men fear: the mouth or womb devouring the phallus.

Since the male characters cannot read her bodily text, she must use male productions such as books, writing, and Latin as a means to speak to her family members. Lavinia blends her female body with the phallic staff and with the masculine hand to appropriate these objects' power in the patriarchy to translate the body's text. She grabs Titus's hand in her mouth; Titus instructs her, "bear thou my hand, sweet wench, between thy teeth" (3.1.282). The hand is the writer.[6] I believe Marie Loughlin is correct when she states that Lavinia's carrying her father's hand in her mouth in 5.1 indicates that the tongue is the site of masculine status and the origin of language (218). In addition, the bodily text of Lavinia is blended here with the discourse of male

---

[6] By asserting that Lavinia's text is translated by taking the hand of Titus in her mouth, I am following the lead of Cixous's statement in "The Laugh of the Medusa" that women must seize patriarchal discourse in their mouths and bite it to write (887).

society, with the language of the writer. In 3.2, Titus and Lavinia retire together so that he can read with her the stories "in times of old" (83). Shakespeare designs this scene to be a blending of "his story" and "her story," a linking of male and female discourse into a "bisexual" text.

Conclusion

> Rare are the men able to venture onto the brink where writing, freed from law, unencumbered by moderation, exceeds phallic authority, and where the subjectivity inscribing its effects becomes feminine. (Cixous, *The Newly Born Woman* 86)

Lavinia's body speaks, because Shakespeare is the kind of writer Cixous speaks of in this epigraph. Shakespeare constructs Lavinia to be invincible; she is the only character who emerges from the pit in 2.4 (the image of the consuming womb in the drama), and lives on. Because of this, she becomes a living sign of the opposing maternal body, one that nurtures. "There is something of the mother in every woman," as Cixous puts it ("Coming" 50). Quintus explains that the hole is "blood-stained" like the site of the female womb. Martius describes the hole as "a very fatal place" (2.3.202) and "a fearful sight of [. . .] death" (2.3.216). Quintus suggests that the pit is a "swallowing womb" (239) and that those in the pit are on the "brink" (241). Because the pit is depicted as a womb, the womb being the generator of a life through birth that always culminates in death, the womb is also "unhallow'd" (210) or a representation of the contaminated maternal body to Martius. Therefore, the birthing process is defined by the male characters as dirty and defiled. Lavinia's presence in the play changes the signification of the pit, as James explains:

> Marcus contributes to the violation of representational norms which Shakespeare condenses in the image of the pit. The pit metamorphically assumes the shapes of Tamora, Lavinia,

Philomela, Dido, Dido's cave, the classical Underworld, and even the Andronici's tomb, the "sacred receptacle" retaining Titus's sons. Marcus's speech identifies both the Ovidian text that will replace Virgil's as the shaping myth of this late Roman society, and the violent poetics that separates decorative signifiers from their gory referents. He also transforms Lavinia's body into an iconographic sign of violation, affecting the literary, rhetorical, cultural, and epistemological reaches of the play: it is the final version of that pit. Her body, inscribed with Philomela's fate, haunts the audiences imagination [. . .] That mutilated, voiceless, but overly signifying body becomes a spectacle that sucks up and annihilates Marcus's golden poetry [. . . the pit and Lavinia's body] simultaneously produce and consume meaning. (64)

In 2.3, Martius notices "a precious ring that lightens all the hole, / [. . .] like a taper in some monument" (2.3.227-28). He refers to a ring on Bassianus's finger but he could well be defining the womb/tomb that Titus discusses in act 1 and the figure of the nurturing maternal body that Lavinia represents in the play. In addition, the light from the ring is compared to the moonlight that shone on Pyramus in legend "when he by night lay bath'd in maiden blood" (2.3.231-32). The blood of Lavinia and of the maternal body anoint the murdered body of Bassianus, his blood mixing with theirs. Her bodily text conveys the mutilation of herself and of her husband, Bassianus, by the patriarchy; she is raped lying on her husband's body. Therefore, her body translates and transports both their texts, their meaning. Instead of disarming or disempowering Lavinia's text in the gang rape and mutilation, Demetrius and Chiron succeed in doing the opposite; Lavinia's bodily text becomes so overwhelming that it makes the patriarchal text that Tamora's sons represent mute.

In the final scene of the drama, Lucius, as the new emperor of Rome, declares that Tamora will have "No funeral rite, nor man in mourning weed, / No mournful bell shall ring her burial, / But throw her forth to beasts and birds to prey: / Her life was beastly and devoid of pity (5.3.196-99). In these final words, Lucius imagines the "ravenous" (5.3.195) and "beastly" (5.3.199) maternal body being ignored and consumed and, in its place, honors Lavinia's bodily text that is enclosed in the Andronici tomb, in the nurturing maternal body that Lucius describes as "our household's monument" (5.3.193-94). Lucius and Marcus' tears and kisses cannot remove the bloodstains from Titus: "O, take this warm kiss on thy pale cold lips, / These sorrowful drops upon thy blood[-stain'd] face" (5.3.153-54). Titus is being committed to the family tomb, returned to the body of mother earth. Titus, like Bassianus earlier in the play, has his blood mixed with that of Lavinia in the Andronici tomb, returning him figuratively to the maternal body.

Shakespeare crafts his characters to indicate that the body's true text cannot be dismembered because it continues to outpour signification of the mother tongue. Marcus relates Lavinia's blood to "a crimson river" (2.4.22) and "a bubbling fountain stirr'd with the wind" (2.4.23) after her mutilation. The blood from her mouth is like the bleeding pit in the previous scene; it is the ink of the female body's text. The female body's text as authorial disgorgement is translated to the page; it is a text that deconstructs the whiteness of the blank page and puts in the place of male constructs a feminine text in blood, like Lavinia's streaming blood (Gajowski 8).

When Lavinia kneels with her family (4.1.87) to swear "mortal revenge" (4.1.93) to see the blood of her attackers (4.1.94), she becomes a collaborator in Titus's plan, not as a mad woman nor as an innocent or unwary victim of her father's madness and rage as she is often interpreted. In 5.1, she enters the feast veiled, as a bride might be or as a handmaiden who is returning to her husband and to the womb/tomb. It is of import to this study that Titus executes his daughter; it indicates his acceptance of the maternal body. If Lavinia had committed suicide, which is alluded to by Titus and Marcus in

3.2.16-22, Shakespeare's interrogation of the female body's text would be incomplete. The love that Titus and Bassianus have for Lavinia helps them to get in touch once again with the mother tongue as well as to see the damaging effects of figurative decapitation on the female body.

Lavinia's death is a requiem for the victimized female body. Even after her body has disappeared from the stage, her bodily text speaks. When Titus kills her in 5.3, her corporeal body completely vanishes in death and what is left alive is the purport representing the body. The image of Lavinia's raped and mutilated figure onstage makes an indelible impression on the audience; it cannot be erased or commodified. For example, the mental picture of her ravaged body that reappears onstage in 2.4 and Lavinia's veiled presence awaiting death at the banquet scene in 5.3 are indelible visual images for the audience.

Pascale Aebischer contends that Lavinia's bodily absence on stage creates a space that is immediately filled by the predominately male cast of characters that overtake the audience's focus causing it to forget the absent victim (5). I completely disagree. Lavinia's "monstrous" presence on stage in six scenes after the rape and mutilation testifies to the illusion of patriarchal power and is an allusion to male linguistic impotence. Therefore, the female body's text is a more powerful sign than anything that men do to inscribe meaning on women.

Titus explains at the outset of the play that the dead bodies of his family in the Andronici tomb speak through silence (1.1.90). This phrase is very telling, since later in the play the text of Lavinia's living, disfigured body and later her slain body will in fact speak in its silence. Titus exhibits the ability to express the disruptive powers of the female bodily text throughout the play but especially in the final scene. He would not be able to translate the female body's text if it were not for all that goes before, if it were not for Lavinia and her outpouring of expression. Titus executes Lavinia in act 5, assisting in producing her body's text that not only speaks through silence but disturbs the silence. "Silence contains all potential sound," in Susan Gubar's words (305).

Disgorgement through the form of the female body's text and using male language to translate this text explodes his story and history, which is based on the oppression of women, and creates her story and *herstory* which is based on the expression of women. *Herstory* is always a tragedy. Lavinia is a "map of woe" (3.2.12), the tragedy of figurative decapitation that men might read, but most of the men in the play aren't able to follow it. Patriarchal rules in the Early Modern era, their expectations inscribed on to women, rape, mute, and mutilate the discourse between the sexes. Lavinia bears on the outside of her body the scars that all women bear on the inside: the decapitating force of oppression, silencing, and marginalization. Titus suggests that her wounds depict *her story* when he tells her, "Thou shalt not sigh, not hold thy stumps to heaven, / Nor wink, nor nod, nor kneel, nor make a sign, / But I, of these, will wrest an alphabet, / And by still practice learn to know thy meaning" (3.2.42-45). To hear the female body's text, a member of the patriarchy must be "still," not immersed in the noise of male language. Titus has begun to embrace the female body's disgorgement. Titus's list of Lavinia's body parts that speak her text, unlike Michel de Montaigne's litany of bodily texts, delineates the story of female figurative decapitation, of the *herstory* of women who have been either physically or figuratively raped by patriarchal constructs. Chapter 3 describes how John Milton uses the bodily text of Eve to reveal his version of the origin of *herstory* by imbuing Eve with the characteristics stereotypically identified with the Virgin Mary.

CHAPTER 3
EVE IN JOHN MILTON'S *PARADISE LOST*

John Milton, like Shakespeare, was interested in how the female body *speaks* its text. For the most part, the male characters in his epic poetry, like Samson, Lycidas, and Adam, are exemplars of restraint and nobility. As Jerome Bump explains, many view Milton as the stern, ascetic Puritan who imbued his poetic characters with these same attributes (324). However, his female characters, like Delilah in *Samson Agonistes*, the Lady and Sabrina in *Comus*, and Eve and Mary in *Paradise Lost* and *Paradise Regained*, are not images of withholding and restraint; they disgorge their text despite being figuratively decapitated by the male characters. The female characters manage to subvert the male texts through their own kind of chaos and exude generosity despite how they are treated by their male counterparts.

Milton has often been accused of exhibiting Ovidian discourse, denigrating women in his writings. However, not all critics, including myself, have agreed with this interpretation. Poets in the nineteenth century like Hazlitt, Keats, Shelley, Wordsworth, and Blake admired Milton's progressive attitudes on political, moral, and social issues. Samuel Taylor Coleridge in 1818 commended Milton's recognition of Adam and Eve's "mutual rationality" and spiritual equality in *Paradise Lost* (96). Mary Wollstonecraft, writing in the 1790s, agreed with Coleridge's viewpoint. In her time, Milton was viewed by women like Charlotte Smith, Catherine Talbot, and Anna Barbauld as an anarchist inciting women to rebel against their suppressed state (Wittreich 6). Wollstonecraft also saw that Milton's Eve was "one of the masculine stereotypes of female nature" and revealed more about the male imagination in Renaissance England and their view of woman as the Puritan housewife than about the bible (13). Wollstonecraft believed he was attempting in *Paradise Lost* to condemn such behavior by men:

"For Milton, a woman was not a mere satellite" (13). Wollstonecraft commended his attempts in his epic poem to try to free women of the "bondage of species," to attempt to show women as the social and cultural equals of men.

It is possible that his female characters exude a markedly different type of text than the male figures Milton creates and that his characterization of Eve in *Paradise Lost* is a critique of the figurative decapitation of women as well as a dialogue on the disgorgement of female text. This chapter takes to task the image of "Milton's bogey" from Virginia Woolf's *A Room of One's Own* discussed in Sandra Gilbert and Susan Gubar's *The Madwoman in the Attic* (188) and presents a different view of Milton's writing of and about women.

Plot Summary

Milton's epic narrative is his vision of the rebellion, the war, and the fall of a faction of angels, lead by Satan, from heaven into hell's depths. In book 2, the fallen angels, burning in hell's flames, debate their next move. It is decided that Satan will leave hell and tempt God's creations on earth to destroy the innocence of Adam and Eve. The description of the beginning of the world and the peaceful, agrarian lives of Adam and Eve is part of the narrative poem. Eve's temptation by Satan, the fall of Adam and Eve, and their banishment from Eden are central to the poem. *Paradise Lost* is the prequel to *Paradise Regained* where the second Eve, Mary, and her son Jesus are described and Jesus is tempted by Satan, just as Eve was as chronicled in *Paradise Lost.*

Figurative Decapitation

> What does he want in return – the traditional man? [. . .] At first what he wants [. . .] is that he gain more masculinity [. . .] Moreover, that is what society is made for – how it is made; and men can hardly get out of it. (Cixous, *The Newly Born Woman* 87)

3. *Eve in Milton's* Paradise Lost

Milton's *Paradise Lost* comments on the gain of masculinity and the figurative decapitation of the feminine in all aspects as a part of that gain. One of the ways in which he discusses this gain of masculinity at the expense of femininity is through the depiction of the classical image of Sin, Satan's daughter. She is depicted as serpentine like Satan (Gilbert and Gubar 197), but she is also described as the essence of monstrous maternity:

> The one seem'd Woman to the waste, and fair,
> But ended foul in many a scaly fould
> Voluminous and vast, a Serpent arm'd
> With mortal sting: about her middle round
> A cry of Hell Hounds never ceasing bark'd
> With wide *Cerberean* mouths full loud, and rung
> A hideous Peal: yet, when they list, would creep,
> If aught disturb'd thir noyse, into her womb,
> And kennel there, yet there still bark'd and howl'd
> Within unseen. (2. 650-69)

Critically, Sin's maternity in Milton's poem has been paralleled with Eve's fall as the catalyst for her "slave[ry] to the species" (Gilbert and Gubar 198). Motherhood, embodied as Sin in *Paradise Lost*, is poisonous as opposed to the nurturing motherhood of the Virgin Mary in *Paradise Regained*. Nurturing versus monstrous maternity is personified by Lavinia and Tamora in *Titus Andronicus* and by Alexandra and Mariam in *The Tragedy of Mariam*, illustrating the binary discourse that is set up in these texts. Women are either chaste or unchaste, holy or sinful.

The figuratively decapitating attitude that women should be silent, obedient, modest and chaste is exemplified in the male figures' attitude towards Eve in Milton's poem. He describes the female place in patriarchal culture: "Hee for God only, shee for God in him: / His fair large Front and Eye sublime declar'd / Absolute rule" (4. 99-301). Eve must worship her husband and obey his will in much the same way that the faithful must have an obedient, patient love of God, in a passive state of waiting, as William Forget indicates (38). She displays "submissive charms" (4.498), happily obeying Adam's will as well as God's law (4.636). The male figures in *Paradise Lost* place her in a position where she must adhere to the stereotyped qualities of being female in a male world. She does not interfere in Adam's conversation with Raphael, because she has been trained that it is not her place to interfere in men's work. Instead of wanting to speak to God's emissary herself, "Her Husband the Relater she preferr'd [. . .] and of him to ask / Chose rather" (8.52-54). Eve overhears Adam's praise of her, and with "Virgin modesty" and unobtrusive nature turns to walk to the "Nuptial Bower," Adam leading her there (8.501-11). Adam admires Eve's "graceful acts, / Those thousand decencies that daily flow / From all her words and actions, mixt with Love / And sweet compliance" (8.600-03). Eve exhibits Cixous's juxtaposition of propriety and property in these lines:

> with eyes
> Of conjugal attraction unreprov'd,
> And meek surrender, half imbracing leand
> On our first Father, half her swelling Breast
> Naked met his under the flowing Gold
> Of her loose tresses hid: he in delight
> Both of her Beauty and submissive Charms. (4.492-98)

This eroticizing of Eve objectifies her; she becomes figuratively decapitated, mere body parts. The woman's body parts are worshipped but the woman herself disappears behind the emphasis on mere physical appearance. Milton critiques Petrarchan discourse by eroticizing Eve's appearance before and after the fall; he also subverts her decapitation by giving her attributes similar to Adam's. She humbly begs Adam's forgiveness (10.912-13, 917), with "reverence in my [Eve's] heart" (915). She also "prostrate fell / before him [God] reverent" and "confess'd / Humbly [her] faults" (099-100). The angel Michael in book

12 has calmed her with dreams and "all her spirit comps'd spelling correct?/ To meek submission" (595-97). Another passage which pertains to the figuratively decapitating attitudes toward women is in book 4, where Eve addresses Adam stating, "My Author and Disposer, what thou bidst / Unargu'd I obey; so God ordains, / God is thy Law, thou mine: to know no more / Is woman's happiest knowledge and her praise" (635-38). She says all the right words and exhibits all the right behaviors for a woman in a male-dominated world.

Yet, Milton makes it clear that Eve is much more than just a meek flower in the garden of Eden. She resembles Adam: both are curious about their place in the universe, both are physically beautiful, both are intelligent, both are caretakers of Eden. Milton creates a disgorgement of text by writing the qualities of similarity and difference into Eve's character not only in relation to Adam, Gabriel, and Satan but to Sin and to the Virgin Mary, a character from the companion piece to *Paradise Lost*, as well. The comparisons are an outpouring of bisexual discourse, finding connections between the female figures and the male characters. The similarities and differences between Eve depicted in *Paradise Lost* and the Virgin Mary from *Paradise Regained* constitute Milton's disgorgement.

Disgorgement

> The woman arriving over and over again does not stand still; she's everywhere, she exchanges, she is the desire-that-gives [. . .] She doesn't know what she's giving, she doesn't measure it; she gives, though, neither a counterfeit impression nor something she hasn't got. She gives more, with no assurance that she'll get back even some unexpected profit from what she puts out. She gives that there may be life, thought, transformation. (Cixous, "Laugh" 893)

Eve embodies the concept of giving that transforms life. Through his depiction of her, Milton discusses chastity as the basis for interpretative power and creativity; in other words, figurative decapitation for women becomes a springboard for disgorgement of text. Woman's capacity to love, console, and purify, emphasized in Milton's poetry, is Cixous's definition of disgorgement. Eve is portrayed by Milton as a woman with innocent intentions, not as the evil seductress she appears to be in Western culture and art. Her disobedience is contrasted with male disobedience that is exemplified early on in *Paradise Lost*, where Satan and the other fallen angels wage war on Heaven and lose.

Subversion of Language

> A feminine text starts on all sides at once [. . .] you might say it 'gives a send-off' [. . .] giving a send-off is generally giving the *signal* to depart [. . .] allowing departure, allowing breaks, 'parts,' partings, separations [. . .] from this we break with the return-to-self, with [. . .] relations ruling the coherence, the identification, of the individual. (Cixous, "Castration" 175)

Eve is separation, parts, parting, incoherence, departure; she is the face of chaos in *Paradise Lost* through her temptation of Adam and by Satan, and the parallels between her and the character Sin. She is an allegorical figure and so is Eve; Sin is a side of Eve or a mirror reflection of Eve like Eve's reflection in the pool in book 4. Both represent the figurative decapitation of women in an oppressive culture; they set the stage for the disgorgement of all women. Women become known in patriarchal cultures as the descendants of the first mother, Eve. Sin is vulnerable to the charms of Satan, opening the gates of Hell in disobedience to God's edict, just as Eve disobeys God's commandment and succumbs to Satan's trickery. Disobedience is the chaotic, subversive quality these two female characters share, set in juxtaposition to their figurative decapitation by male society.

Sin's and Eve's texts are connected to the text of Chaos. Satan travels through Chaos when he leaves Hell to get to Eden; Sin is guarding the Gate that holds back Chaos. Sin's text is *entredeux*; in book 2, Sin moves between her son, Death, and her father, Satan, to stop them from warring against each other. The dialogue Milton gives to Sin is written in parallel form:

> Fast by Hell Gate, and kept the fatal Key,
> Ris'n, and with hideous outcry rush'd between.
> O Father, what intends thy hand, she cry'd,
> Against thy only Son, What fury O Son,
> Possesses thee to bend that mortal Dart
> Against they fathers Head? (727-30).

The "Hell Gate," that "infernal Vale" (742) where Sin resides is situated in between Hell and the Heaven of Eden. Milton's interrogates the conflict of idealizing and denigrating women, the daughters of Eve, by re-envisioning the myth of Athena who was born from the head of Jove; in Milton's version Sin has "sprung" from Satan's head and Eve was created from Adam's side. Eve's story (the original sin of eating the fruit from the tree of the knowledge of good and evil, bringing birthing and death into the world as punishment for her sin, and giving birth to Cain as another signification of death) is paralleled with the story of the birth of the goddess of wisdom and with the birth of Satan's daughter, Sin, who then gives birth to Satan's son, Death. In this way, Milton uses figurative representations of beauty, wisdom, sin, and death to illustrate that the stereotyping of women has also been born from the mind of man.

Through language, men have created a "false birth" leaving women branded and in eternal torment like the image of Sin in the epic poem: "Here in perpetual agonie and pain, / With terrors and with clamors compasst round / Off mind own brood, that own my bowels feed: / Thou [Satan] are my Father, thou my Author" (2.861-64). Sin is condemned to exist in chaos due to the texts and laws that are born of a male figure in *Paradise Lost*. However, Sin is depicted by Milton as using her chaos to create a textual disgorgement. She is the keeper of the key to the Gate of Hell. The key as phallic symbol is Sin's implement used to "write" her own text; she usurps the text written about her by men by using "the key of this infernal Pit" (2.850). By opening the Gate, Sin lets out "Chaos," "Anarchie," and Lust, "the hoarie deep, a dark / Illimitable Ocean without bound" (2. 891-92).

This description is remiscent of the description of the pit in *Titus Andronicus*. Just as Demetrius and Chiron strive unsuccessfully to individuate from their mother, Tamora, and Titus fears and then comes to embrace the "womb" of the family tomb in Shakespeare's *Titus Andronicus*, Milton gives substance to these fears in his depiction of the hounds of hell as they try to free themselves from the womb of Sin (2.795-803). Satan, like the male characters in *Titus Andronicus*, must surrender himself to the void, "this wild Abyss, / The Womb of nature and perhaps her Grave / Of neither Sea, nor Shore, nor Air, nor Fire, / But all these in thir pregnant causes mixt / Confus'dly" (2.910-14), "a vast vacuitie [. .] Ten thousand fadom deep" (2.932-24).

Eve separates Adam from his promise to God not to taste the fruit of the tree of knowledge of good and evil. The tree itself is discussed in the bible as representing a binary system that Milton's poem complicates. Eve's figurative decapitation due to her association with Sin and with Satan is interrogated through Milton's subversion of the binaries of good and evil: the poet centers on the normal associations in contrast between Eve and "the second Eve," the Virgin Mary, by giving Eve in *Paradise Lost* all the attributes that are connected historically to the Virgin Mary. The best example of duality that is transformed by Milton into a dissertation on *differance* is the scene in which Eve spies her image in the pool in the garden of Eden and admires her own loveliness in *Paradise Lost* (4.455-80).

The similarities and differences between Eve and Mary's characters in Milton's two companionate poems are like Eve's reflection in the pool. Her reflection subverts the typical qualities associated with Eve; the good Eve and the bad Eve look at each other in the pool's surface. Adam's vision of Abel and Cain in book 12 is another example of this reflection: the good brother and the bad brother. In a sense, Eve gives birth to good and to evil. She is obedient and disobedient in *Paradise Lost*. The poet deconstructs the binary opposition of evil and good, disobedience and obedience; the line between purity and sin is very thin, as thin as the surface of the pond Eve sees her image in. "Eve's relation to Adam as mirror and shadow is the paradigmatic relations which canonical authority institutes between itself and its believers, converting them [. . .] to a 'higher authority,'" as Annabel Patterson explains (150). One of the ways Milton achieves this subversion of text is through emphasizing the twin natures of Eve and Mary. Sister Mary Christopher Pecheux states that the author's study of the pairing of Eve and Mary in *Paradise Lost* "reveals nothing basically new" (366). I disagree. Milton connects the lost and regained paradise of mankind which he explains in the first 5 lines of book 1 of *Paradise Lost* and in the first 7 lines of book 1 of *Paradise Regained* through the twin characters of Eve and Mary, and Milton creates an Eve legend that uplifts the denigrating characterization of the mother of mankind as a temptress and Mary antitype (Jolly 35) by demonstrating within Eve the extolled virtues of Mary.

By doing this, Milton creates a disgorgement of text by deconstructing the body as text attached to Eve and Mary. Milton generates a version of Eve that was unprecedented in seventeenth-century poetry; a dichotomy between Eve and Mary was a common perception in medieval and Renaissance religious doctrine, as Elise Lawton Smith observes (296). The characterization of Eve as an antitype to Mary is prevalent in literature "from Ambrose and Augustine to Luther and Kierkegaard" as Sally Cunneen indicates (17). Mosaics from twelfth and thirteenth century churches in Italy (Monreale, Torcello, and Murano) display Eve as Mary's antitype. These mosaics stress Eve's susceptibility to temptation, her pride leading to disobedience, and her carnal desire for Adam, according to Penny Howell Jolly (35). These qualities are opposed in the mosaics to Mary's reception of archangel Gabriel, her humble obedience to God, and her conception of Christ through the Word. "Where Mary is the rose, Eve is the thorn" as Jolly observes (61). Milton was certainly aware of this dichotomy and creates a disgorgement of text through merging the texts of Mary and Eve.

Maurice Hamington points out that Eve and Mary have been portrayed as polar opposites throughout history. Eve stands for disobedience, sorrow, darkness, sin, the Fall, condemnation, death, paradise lost, cooperation with Satan, and sexuality whereas Mary represents obedience, joy, light, salvation, restoration, praise, life, paradise gained, cooperation with God, and virginity (137). Milton re-creates the duality of Eve and Mary in his version of the Eve myth. Sister Mary Pecheux is correct when she states that Irenaeus was in error when he expostulated that Mary's character absorbs Eve (366). The two figures merge in Milton's poetry.

Eve is connected to Mary in a variety of manners and methods in *Paradise Lost*. Gabriel uses the words "Hail Mary" at the Annunciation; on Eve "the Angel *Hail* / Bestow'd, the holy salutation us'd / Long after to blest *Mary*, second *Eve*" (5.385-87). The poet ties Eve to the "second Eve," Mary, again in book 10 (83). In particular, Adam connects Eve and Mary in chapter 10 and 12. Through re-creating the image of Eve in his poetry, Milton deconstructs the binary system of thought where she is the fallen woman and Mary is the innocent woman.

Mary's virtues are extolled in *Paradise Regained*, which are magnified in Milton's depiction of Eve in *Paradise Lost*. Mary is a virgin of virtue; her virgin birth is explained by God in book 1 of *Paradise Regained* (134-40) and by Christ in book 1 (238-9). Mary's humility, obedience, and faith in God are also praised in book 1 (235-40). Her purity is acclaimed in book 2 (63). Though troubled when Christ does not return immediately from the baptism in book 2, Mary displays humility, patience, compassion, faithfulness, simplicity, and domesticity. She is depicted waiting faithfully at home for her son's return at the very end of book 4. She has "meekly compos'd awaited the fulfilling" of Christ's mission on earth (108). She has become "inur'd" "to wait with patience" (102). Mary's courage through patience is weighted equally to Christ's courage in the face of Satan's temptation. She humbly accepts her fate and her role in the redemption. She has acquiesced to the burden she carries (93-94); Mary exhibits temperance.

Milton takes these characteristics of Mary and amplifies them in his portrayal of Eve. An example of this expansion is seen in the temptation scenes of Eve and Mary. Mary is puzzled by God's ways in book 2 of *Paradise Regained*; Eve exhibits this quality as well as Herbert Petit argues (367). Both women have a test of faith just as Christ does in *Paradise Regained*, and yet Mary's faith is tested in only 50 lines of book 2 (58-108). In *Paradise Lost*, Eve must prove her obedience, faithfulness and trust in Adam and in God again and again: in book 4 when she views her reflection in the pool of water (461-91) "and though she is seduced by it, she chooses to be with Adam," as George F. Butler observes (166), in 4.635-39 when she obeys Adam's instructions, in 4.800-09 and in book 4.28-93 when she is unsettled by her dream of Satan's temptation, in book 5.320-49 when she retires from the scene to allow Raphael and Adam conference in private, and in book 9 where Satan tempts her hunger and vanity (much in the way he tempts Christ in *Paradise Regained*) for 238 lines until she finally succumbs (532-780). Eve in *Paradise Lost* is paralleled with Christ in *Paradise Regained*; both have their virtue tested by Satan.

In *Paradise Lost*, Eve embodies the qualities of beauty, elegance, innocence, simplicity, fidelity, humility, domesticity, piety, patience, and compassion – all qualities that are usually attributed to the Virgin Mary. The archangel Michael in book 12 of *Paradise Lost* states that if one has "Faith...Virtue, Patience...Charity," then one will "possess a paradise within thee, happier far" (582-7). Milton's Eve embodies this kind of paradise. Milton begins with an emphasis of her "perfect beauty" in 4.634, her "sweet attractive Grace" (4.298). Satan relates that she has a "Divine resemblance" (4.364). She is described in *Paradise Lost* as "fair" in books 4, 5, 8, and 9. "Satan's flattery of Eve's beauty (book 9) [. . .] is roughly equivalent to Gabriel's praise of Mary"

(Pecheux 363). Eve is characterized as having "In every gesture dignity and love" (8.488). In a miniature painted by Berthold Furtmeyer in 1481 called *Tree of Death and Life*, Eve and Mary are depicted as twins, their faces being identical, as Anne Baring and Jules Cashford indicate (573).

Eve's innocence is an important part of her characterization. In *Paradise Lost*, Eve's "*Virgin* Majesty" and faithfulness is defined (9.270, 320). Eve's deportment is outlined as "Goddess-like" (9.389) and humble. Her virginity is often interpreted by critics to indicate her innocence rather than her sexual inexperience. The use of capitalization on certain words like the word *virgin* tie Eve to Mary in the two poems. Eve discusses her innocent nature in 4.457, and Milton praises her virtue in prayer in 5.209. Her virtuous nature in her nakedness before God and God's messenger Raphael is extolled (5.384).

Satan notices Eve's "Nymphlike step," her virginity, sweetness, grace and innocence (9.452-59) as well as her beauty (9.489, 540). Satan plays upon her innocence, "our credulous Mother," in the temptation scene in *Paradise Lost* (9.644). In fact, there is a grouping of references to her virginity in book 9 (270, 396, 411, 900) to emphasize her innocence in the face of temptation which appears nowhere else in the poem as Pecheux remarks (361). "Eve is flowerlike in her loveliness and also in her moral and sexual innocence," according to Kathleen M. Swaim (164). Her sweetness and amiability is presented in the explanation of the creation of Adam and Eve in book 8 (475, 484) and in Adam's lament of the temptation in 9.899. This parallel connects the creation to the fall which will later be redeemed when Mary bears the Christ child. Adam displays his belief in Eve's "native innocence" and "virtue" in 9.373-74. She expresses joy in the simplicity of Eden with Adam in book 4 (337, 646).

In addition to Eve's innocence, her faithfulness is delineated in several passages of Milton's *Paradise Lost*. The precedent for her fidelity can be found in the New Testament description of Mary. When Joseph follows the angel's warning and flees to Egypt in Matthew 2.14,

Mary takes Jesus and willingly obeys her husband and their spiritual guide. Later, in 2.21, when Joseph is commanded in a dream to take Mary and Jesus to Israel, Mary again follows her husband without question. In like manner, Eve in Milton's poem pledges obedience to God's will concerning prohibition of the fruit of the Tree of Knowledge (4.444) and returns to Adam, leaving the temptation of her own reflection in the pool, accepting with faith the wishes of the voice of God (4.489). Milton describes Eve's acquiescence here as "meek surrender" (4.494); in this same way, Mary is faithful to the word of God and takes on the responsibility of bearing the Christ child.

Adam praises Eve by calling her "accomplisht" (4.660). She is "pious" and remorseful in response to her dream (5.135). Eve, with meekness and humility, replies to Adam about her unworthiness to be the "mother of mankind" (9.162). She is portrayed as industrious and domestic as she gently tends the garden in Eden (5.136; 9.214, 430; 11.171). In paintings of the Annunciation, Mary is often depicted reading or sewing. Eve nurtures the garden as if it is her "Nursery" (8.46); this domesticity in her also reveals her "Majestic [. . .] Grace" (42-3) and humility.

There are many examples of Eve's piety and humility in *Paradise Lost* which relate to corresponding illustrations of Mary's reverence in the New Testament Gospel according to Luke. When Gabriel initially brings Mary the news of her virgin birth, she says in chapter 1.38: "I am the servant of the Lord. Let it be done to me as you say." In "Mary's Canticle" in chapter 1.46, she pronounces her devotion to God: "My being proclaims the greatness of the Lord, my spirit finds joy in God my savior." Likewise, Eve is prayerful, thankful to God for his goodness in several passages of *Paradise Lost* (9.198, 721; 5.145). She admits with humble shame her part in the fall of man in book 10 (159-61).

In addition, Milton's *Paradise Lost* and *Paradise Regained* reveal Eve as not only a reflection of Mary's positive qualities, superimposing the text of these two characters and deconstructing historical texts that see the two characters as opposites, but by doing this Milton also merges Eve's text with Adam, and Satan's discourse showing her to have the strength and power of her male counterparts and merges her text with historical male writings that show Eve and Mary to have twin natures.

Jouissance **through Bisexual Discourse**

> Female writing is a translation between body and text, "working (in) the in-between, inspecting the process of the same and of the other [. . .] to admit this is first to want the two, as well as both, the ensemble of the one and the other [. . .] an incessant process of exchange from one subject to another." (Cixous "Laugh" 883)

Milton's subversion of text in *Paradise Lost* is at the same time his display of *jouissance* in discourse. His Eve is a complex portrait personifying the female text as a discourse of exchange between same and other, exhibiting the nobility and power of his Adam and Satan as well as the stereotypic and opposing feminine qualities of lust and monstrous maternity versus passivity and patience. Joan Mallory Webber believes that Milton was a "modernist" whose poem was preparing the way for feminist thinking because his poem was an appeal to the victimized (6). The "politics of reading the patriarchal canon" holds up "the ideals of 'thinking like a man'" (Patterson 21). Actually, thinking like a man and like a woman, the oppressor and the oppressed, are melded in *Paradise Lost*, especially in the character, Eve. She is a mirror of Satan; Eve and Satan suffer from the sin of pride. Instead of seeing Adam as her reflection, modeling herself after him, Eve sees her own reflection in the pool in book 4. Milton deconstructs the idea that women must be a reflection of male society's set of virtues. The passage in *Paradise Lost* where Eve sees her reflection in the pool also joins Eve's text with the classical test of Narcissus who also saw his reflection in the pool. Both Eve and Narcissus "drown" in their own hubris.

3. Eve in Milton's Paradise Lost

Milton's Eve is based on the sources of Genesis, Anderini's *L'Adama*, Peyton's *Glass of Tome*, and Beaumont's *Psyche* (Hutcherson 28). Therefore, Milton's Eve is an amalgamation of stereotypical masculine and feminine texts. She is inferior in the hierarchal structure, but the harmony in Eden, the mutual respect, loyalty and obligation, is emphasized just as much as the hierarchy. An example of this is in book 4 where the poet describes "our two first Parents" as

> Two of far nobler shape erect and tall,
> Godlike erect, with native Honour clad
> In naked Majestie seemd Lords of all,
> And worthie seemd,
> for in thir looks Divine
> The image of thir glorious Maker shon. (288-92)

This description of Adam and Eve is equal; it indicates no superiority in delineating Adam.

Milton's syntax is not derogatory toward Eve but embodies the mutual need between the sexes. She is defined in book 8 not in subordinate terms but as "societie" and "companie" for Adam (444-51). Barbara K. Lewalski asserts that the interdependence and powerful bonding of Adam and Eve reveals Milton's complex treatment of women in his poem (11). Eve participates in Milton's Eden in the full range of human activities; the author paints her with qualities that are exceptional for his time. Adam and Eve are both held individually responsible for their actions.

Adam is actually viewed by some critics as more culpable than Eve for the fall of mankind since his connection to "right reason" was supposed to help him lead her to the path of righteousness (12.84). Therefore, Adam is seen as the greater transgressor as Philip Gallegher professes (128). Adam can be viewed as the actual cause of the fall, because there are numerous references in books 5, 8, and 9 to his unquenchable desire for knowledge and ascension to a higher plane in the hierarchy. One place in Milton's poem where this is revealed is in 6.908-09. Adam is instructed in this manner: "But list'n not to his Temptations, warn/Thy weaker." In this last line, Eve is also figuratively *decapitated* as the weaker entity, Adam being the stronger of the two. Milton is revealing the past propensity to interpret the stories in the bible as oppressing women. However, the bible can also be read as expounding the strengths of women like Ruth and Sara.

The author's works also reveal this duality, this combination of stereotypical male and female attributes within the female characters that he pens; Delilah in *Samson* Agonistes, Eve in *Paradise Lost*, and Mary in *Paradise Regained* are good examples of this *jouissance* through binary text. Wendy Furman describes Milton's Eve as vulnerable but not weak, powerful but not threatening, life-giving and redemptive. The temptation of Eve by Satan is reminiscent of the temptation of Christ by Satan in Milton's *Paradise Regained*. The author's poetry deconstructs the binary system of language ascribed to women, in particular Petrarchan versus Ovidian discourse about women. The idealization of Mary is merged with the text of Eve and the denigration of her as associated with the character Sin is connected to Adam and Satan's discourse.

Milton's *Paradise Lost* is a re-visionary critique of other authorial and artistic models; the concept of linking Eve to Mary has many archetypal origins. There is a sisterhood that appears in many texts about Mary and Eve, including Milton's epic poems. His text joins male and female texts: his own poem and the historic books and artworks created by male authors and artists connected to the texts and art of female writers and artists as they ponder the bodily texts of Eve and Mary. Second-century theologian Justin Martyr was the first writer to introduce the concept of Mary as the second Eve in section 3 of *Dialogus cum Tryphone* as C.A. Patrides notes (132). In this passage, Justin Martyr compares Eve and Mary as they receive the Word of evil and of salvation during the temptation and in the Annunciation, respectively.[7]

In addition, the critical pairing of the scene of the temptation of Eve and of Mary's Annunciation appears as early as the third century in the writings of Tertullian as Hamington chronicles (128). Shawcross indicates that the ear is also seen by critics as a symbol of the womb, linking Eve's motherhood to Mary's (202). Yrjo Hirn in his book *The Sacred Shrine* indicates that in one tradition, the Virgin Mary asked herself whether Gabriel's pronouncement at the Annunciation "did not threaten some misfortune, like the promise given to the mother of her race by the serpent" as A.B. Chambers discusses (190). Milton was cognizant of many different readings of scripture. Wendy Furman reveals that Mary Elizabeth Groom, a British engraver, illustrated an edition of *Paradise Lost* published in 1937, and in her depiction of the Fall, Eve is surrounded by Mary's flower, the rose (150). In Groom's illustration, Eve is disquieted by Satan's salutation and approach much as Mary is portrayed in Annunciation scenes created by Botticelli and Lippo Lippi. Beth Williamson explains that "O felix culpa" (O lucky fault) in the Exultel hymn for Easter Eve relates to the parallel between Eve and Mary as Beth Williamson explains (1).

The connection of Eve and Mary also appears in artwork from the Middle ages and from the Renaissance. Ernst Guldan in his book *Eva und Maria* chronicles approximately 175 artistic pairings of Eve and Mary continuing throughout and past Milton's lifetime, the earliest depiction occurring in 1015 as Roland Mushat Frye explores (275).

---

[7] Zeno, the bishop of Verona in the late fourth century, refers to the seduction and the redemption of Mary and Eve through language, articulated in Maurice Hamington's *Hail Mary? The Struggle for Ultimate Womanhood in Catholicism* (135). The scene of Eve's temptation is linked to Mary's Annunciation also in the late 13th-century *Biblia Pauperum* according to Penny Jolly in *Made in God's Image? Eve and Adam in the Genesis Mosaics at San Marco, Venice.*

Barbara Grizzuti Harrison describes one depiction of Eve and Mary as twins: "On the doors of the Baptistery in Florence, Ghilberti has sculpted Eve and Mary. He sees them, beautifully, as twins. Arms entwined, they ascend, together, into heaven. What this tells us is that sinlessness and imperfection are braided" (56). In the 1432 rendering entitled "The Annunciation" by Fra Angelico, the wing tips of the angel giving the news to Mary cut into the picture of Adam and Eve's expulsion from the Garden of Eden. "The eye cannot rest with either Mary or Adam and Eve, but alternating between them, finally acknowledge their relationship" (Baring and Cashford 538).

Milton would have been aware of religious artwork pairing Eve and Mary. The stained glass window created at Saint Vincent in Rouen, France around 1525 demonstrates a triumphal procession in which the "history of the Fall and the Redemption" are connected as Emile Male observes (138). In the first panel, Adam and Eve are depicted in an earthly paradise conveyed by a golden chariot attended by the Virtues, and in the third panel, the Virgin Mary is seated in the chariot as "the regenerate Eve," joined by angels, prophets, and patriarchs. Dutch painter Lucas Van Leyden's triptych *The Dance Around the Golden Calf* depicts Israelite mothers in the side panels whose actions "span the distance from Eve to Mary" according to Elise Lawton Smith (311). Their presence in the triptych symbolize the redemptive powers of motherhood in Eve and in the "second Eve." Juxtaposed   words   are joined together in *Paradise Lost*. A definite connection between *Paradise Lost* and medieval religious art is tied in the concept of "fruit of thy womb." In one of the Italian paintings of Eve and of Mary in the late fourteenth and early fifteenth centuries, Eve sits at the feet of Mary; Eve is holding the fruit in her hands in the same way that Mary is depicted holding the baby Jesus as Williamson discusses (1). In *Paradise Lost*, Adam comforts Eve by reminding her that her pain in childbirth will be "soon recompens't with joy, Fruit of thy Womb" (10. 1053). In chapter 1 of the Gospel according to Luke, Elizabeth addresses Mary as "Blest are you among women and blest is the fruit of your womb." The Catholic prayers "The Hail, Holy Queen" and "The Hail Mary" both refer to "fruit of thy womb, Jesus." Milton parallels Eve's eating of the fruit in the original sin and the fruit of Eve's womb that will through the generations be tied to the fruit of Mary's womb, Christ, who will redeem the original fall.

Milton describes the vine and elm as wedded like Eve and Adam in *Paradise Lost* (5.215); the fruitlessness of Eve's sin will ultimately bring about the fruition of Mary's pregnancy and the birth of Christ, often called "the fruitful vine." "Our Mother Eve" (624) realizes in book 12 that although she and Adam have caused the fall, that "By mee the Promis'd Seed shall all restore" (623). Michael reveals the protevangelium to Adam as well in 12.600-02. "Eve's ambition for God-head" is fulfilled by "the later Eve who is to be the instrument of a hypostatic union"; Eve wants to be like God and Mary confesses she is the handmaid of the Lord as Sister Pecheux indicates (363). The poet's idea that the seed of Eve and Mary will bruise the head of the serpent comes from Genesis 3.15, as Hamington argues (127).

Milton conveys a *jouissance* through bisexual discourse by discussing the linking of Eve and Mary through the protevangelium, the idea of the connection of the seed of Eve and Mary which will reek vengeance on Satan's prideful usurpation of Eve's innocence ["the bait of *Eve*/Us'd by the Tempter" (10.551-52)], several times in *Paradise Lost* (10.181, 1031-32; 11.116, 155; 12.148-50, 233-34, 327, 382, 543, 600-02, 623-24) and in *Paradise Regained* (1.54-5, 64-65, 150-53). James Hillman in his *Anima: An Anatomy of a Personified Notion* believes that Milton's connection of Eve and Mary through the protevangelium demonstrates the spiritual tie between Eve and Mary (Shawcross 220). The characteristics shared by Eve and Mary bring about the birth of charity, Christ's forgiveness for a sinful world. Both Eve and Mary are connected because they are both the "Daughter of God and Man" (4.660), and they are contrasted in this case with Sin who is solely the daughter and bride of Satan. Here are two human mothers whose paired natures of lost innocence (Eve) and faithfulness (Mary) redeem through the birth of Christ the original sin of disobedience.

Conclusion

> Now if you are a woman, you are always nearer to and farther from loss than a man is. More and less capable of loss. More attracted, more repulsed. More seduced, more forbidden. (Cixous "Coming to Writing" 39)

Milton's Eve is the archetype of Cixous's definition of loss. Her loss due to the fall is discussed in depth in chapter 12 of *Paradise Lost*. Eve's loss is paralleled with Mary's loss when Christ grows up and leaves home more and more in *Paradise Regained* and then ultimately is crucified as revealed in the *New Testament*. Milton was familiar with different versions of the bible and knew of the different ways Eve and Mary were portrayed. Milton "was not committed to a particular translation [. . .] what Milton uniquely did among seventeenth-century's great religious poets was to become as far as possible a biblical poet himself, not reproducing the language but reconstituting the themes, genres, and stylistic figures of Scripture within his own religious poetry," as Mary Ann Radzinowicz demonstrates (204). Milton, therefore, builds his own Eve mythology. His depiction of Eve is a creation of *herstory* within *history*.

Her bodily text in *Paradise Lost* is an outpouring of the characteristics that are stereotypically associated with the Virgin Mary. Milton's merged text is a disgorgement that deconstructs the dichotomy of Eve as antitype to the Virgin Mary and the connection of Eve to the monstrous maternity of Milton's character Sin, thus *speaking* to Cixous's theory of female libidinal economy.

Shakespeare's Tamora and Lavinia and Cary's Salome and Mariam are characterized as women of opposite natures who actually have overlapping qualities; these are other forms of merged text used to discuss the outpouring of loss and generosity that is the female body's disgorgement. Cary was wrestling with the disparity between acceptable speech for women in private and public arenas; Shakespeare and Milton also touch upon this subject. As is indicated in chapter 4, Isabella Whitney's poetry is imbued with the same propensity toward deconstructing binary oppositions in language as is apparent in *Paradise Lost.*

CHAPTER 4
THE POETRY OF ISABELLA WHITNEY

Isabella Whitney, like Elizabeth Cary, was interested in women's speech and writing. Born into the landed gentry, she used rhetoric in her poetry to negotiate conformity and non-conformity. Her use of syntax deflected negative attention that might surround the non-conformity of her life and attitudes by making it appear that she was conforming to societal constraints on women and on authors. Her apologies and other strategies of veiled discourse in her poetry were used to create a counterfeit persona or narrative voice that covered up authorial disgorgement. Whitney chose to subvert societal dictates by disguising her societal criticism within acceptable forms of private writing for women like family letters and wills, just as Mary Sidney used her version of the psalms for the same purposes.

Public literature about private life with a didactic and grave overtone was a popular writing genre produced by male and female writers of the aristocracy in Tudor England. A clever device that Whitney used in this regard was that the speaker in her poetry was always identified as "Isabella Whitney," thereby presenting all of her poetry as genuinely personal reflection. "Copy of a Letter, Lately written in metre, by a young Gentlewoman: to her unconstant lover" is a poem written by Whitney in 1567 that takes male figures from history like Aeneas, Theseus, and Jason to task for being unfaithful to their devoted lovers. Whitney's narrator in *Copy of a Letter* hints at this profession of ideas for the masses through private forms:

> And when you shall this letter have
> let it be kept in store:
> For she that sent it hath sworne the same,
> as yet to send no more.

And now farewell, for why at large
  my mind is here exprest.
The which you may perceive, if that
  you do peruse the rest. (109-16)[8]

The poet's veiled discourse is often made manifest in puns. The narrator's mind "at large [. . .] exprest" can be read as "largely" or "mostly" but can also indicate Whitney's purpose of speaking to a wider, more public audience. In other words, she is expressing her mind "at large" or for the masses. The narrator swears she will send no more letters to her "unconstant lover," but Whitney appears to be enticing her readership to "peruse the rest" of her work at the same time. "The Manner of Her Will, and What She Left to London and to all Those in it at her Departing" and "An Order Prescribed by Isabella Whitney to Two of her Younger Sisters Serving in London," from the book *A Sweet Nosegay*, are two other poems of Whitney's constructed as personal documents, a will and a letter, and they explain life in London for women of the gentry. These two poems discuss "unconstant lovers" just as *Copy of a Letter* does, so the author does "send more" in 1573.

This is not the only instance in her poetry where her narrator seems to be telling her readership to do one thing while at the same time encouraging them in another direction. Whitney knew her text would be read by a female and male audience, the male audience behaving as voyeurs of female territory, as Ana Kothe asserts (20), so Whitney wanted to *appear* to be conforming to standards set down by male-governed society. Therefore, the use of the word *store* has significance here. She uses this word in many of her poems, extensively in "The Manner of Her Will," and on the surface, Whitney's narrator in *Copy*

---

[8] Quotations of Isabella Whitney's poetry, except *Copy of a Letter*, are from Randall Martin's book entitled *Women Writers in Renaissance England*. Quotations of *Copy of a Letter* are from Betty Travitsky's *Paradise of Women: Writings by Englishwomen of the Renaissance*.

of a Letter urges the faithless lover to keep her letter safe and hidden. However, *store* to the poet also reflects the male world of economy, storing or withholding, versus the world of a woman in the gentry which encompasses a "store" of generosity and giving linked to the feminine body, especially those women in service to the aristocracy. Letters are given to others, but the men in Whitney's period contain female speech and writing. The poem "To her Brother Brooke Whitney" attempts to reinforce the relationship between the narrator and her brother; in the poem, the narrator asks her brother to write to her and see her more often. Whitney alludes to public versus private dialogue again in this poem: "As you shall know; for I will show / You more when we do speak / Than will I write or yet recite / Within this paper weak" (21 24). The author uses the modesty topos to apologize for the "weak" writing of a woman of her station, but the narrator also articulates that public writing in the form of a letter was not the proper place for a woman to reveal a depth of content and intimacy compared to a private conversation between family members. Aristocratic women like Cary and women of the gentry like Whitney were not supposed to put on a public display, either in the theatres or in the realm of publishing, through writing. However, Whitney holds the distinction of being the first Englishwoman to publish a book of poems. She is "the first Englishwoman who writes and publishes in the hope of earning money" as Randall Martin indicates; in so doing, she is "remarkably pioneering" (279).

She was also the first woman of her time, moreover, to criticize men in her poetry, as in *Copy of a Letter,* as Tina Krontiris maintains (33). The poet explains in the poem "An Order Prescribed by Isabella Whitney" that her purpose in writing and publishing is to use her life and pen, a merging of female and male discourses through the joining of the female body as text with the pen(is), to frame an erudite example for all to witness (38). Men may control the pen in her world, but women like Whitney can manipulate the pen(is) that "draws" women, a pen that simultaneously inscribes and attracts. The pen dictates female identity and behavior in Early Modern England but also attracts women like Whitney to use the pen to illustrate her view of female life.

Summary

In "The Manner of Her Will," Whitney develops her narrative voice and poetic form through a poem that is a fictional testament. The narrator of the poem wills all that she owns to the city of London and speaks of London in the poem as if the city is a lover who has spurned her. The narrator's "bequests" are an enumeration and description of the London streets and buildings during the time period when Whitney was living there. The narrator describes a town and people of plenty in a festive tone of voice, but the poem is ironic in nature and is actually a criticism of social ills, including the prison system and health care institutions, and examines the dark lives of those who are destitute. The narrator's amiable affection for the city is offset by the grim description of the lives of the lower classes. Whitney's knowledge of the city of London is extensive and is displayed in the specific details of the poem.

Figurative Decapitation

> [There is] a particular relationship between two economies: a masculine economy and a feminine economy [. . .] an order that works by inculcation, by education: it's always a question of education. An education that consists of [. . .] the force history keeps reserved for woman, the 'capital' force that is effectively decapitation. (Cixous, "Castration" 163)

Whitney's poetry compares and ridicules the male economy in Early Modern England of containing, ordering, and commodifying everything to the female economy of patiently giving, economies that were taught to the people in her time. The male economy is about figuratively *decapitating* women, controlling their identity and sexuality, a major theme in Whitney's writing. Women were expected to emulate the virtues of the Virgin Mary; as Elaine Beilin illustrates, "a good woman was pious, humble, constant, and patient, as well as obedient, chaste, and silent" (*Redeeming Eve* xix).

Women living in Early Modern England were figuratively *decapitated*; they were forced to exhibit these qualities. Having no head to think for herself, the Early Modern woman in England was told who she was and how she was to behave. Being forced to display virtuous characteristics takes away the individual personality of each woman, something that the author protests in her poetry. Whitney, the writer, was not silent, not obedient, and not modest. She shares these attributes with Cary's fictional creation, Mariam. Public display, as in Whitney's publication of her works, was unacceptable behavior, especially for a woman born into the gentry. She had to offset her outspoken and inappropriate behavior through the use of self-effacing techniques, manipulating patriarchal expectations of women to her advantage. "The customary apology which attributes the imperfections of a work to the sex of its author is usually one indication of the constraints felt by women writers," as Krontiris explicates (28).

In addition, women like Whitney needed the financial support and protection of male family members and/or aristocratic patrons. Her poetry reveals the figuratively *decapitating* effects of this dependence of women in her social strata. In "To her Brother Geoffrey Whitney," the narrator discusses the need for financial as well as emotional connections between siblings, especially the loneliness for a single woman separated from her family because they are all working as servants in various households. The poetic narrator explains in "An Order" that women of the gentry in Early Modern Britain must exile "all wanton toys," female pleasures, from their lives (12). Stoic behavior was privileged. With God's help, women were also expected to shield themselves from sexual advances, especially from the master of the household for whom women servants worked. "God shield you from all such as would by word or bill / Procure your shame" (21-22).

Women were supposed to appear to be modest and gentle (27), and women of the gentry in service were also expected to be trustworthy (23, 41).

The author uses societal conventions for women in her poetry to criticize patriarchal treatment of women. Stanza 4 of "An Order" explains the purpose of the entire poem, to "devise" a plan of outward behavior as a survival tactic, a resistance to the abuse that women in service received while employed in artistocratic households:

> Of laughter be not much, nor over solemn seem,
> For then be sure they'll count you light or proud will you
>   esteem,
> Be modest in a mean, be gentle unto all,
> Though cause they give of contrary, yet be to wrath no thrall.
>
> (25-28)

The author depicts female servants as guardians of the household (41-42) who serve God rather than man. However, in the society in which she lived, men had usurped God's place.

Sometime in the late 1560s, Whitney was in service to a London household where part of her duties included housekeeping; "Manual labor of this kind was mandated for any unmarried woman from fourteen to forty by the 1563 State of Artificers, in an effort to cut down on vagabonds," as Ann Rosalind Jones reveals ("Apostrophes to Cities" 156). Although Whitney was employed as an indentured servant, her poetry frees her from the constraints put upon a woman in her station. London is depicted as a faithless man in two of her poems; "An Order . . ." *speaks* to the issue of women serving untrustworthy men instead of God. The poet's "order" *speaks* to the hierarchy of command. Women are "ordered" in Early Modern Britain by men, but Whitney's writing is subversive because she is creating "an order." She "prescribes" a different commander, God, for women to serve in her poem. The word *prescribed* also connotes healing, and her poems often allude to avoiding infection. She intends her poetry as a healing force that subverts infection from the *decapitating* effects of Early Modern English patriarchy: "But this I know, too many live that would [London] soon infect / If God do not prevent, or with his grace expel" (14-15). There are those who would "infect" women if these women are not careful.

Again and again in her poetry, the poet refers to the act of writing. In "An Order" she speaks of writing five times. Writing inoculates her against the infection, and she writes in the hope that her words also inoculate other women against figurative decapitation: "I cannot speak or write too much because I love you well" (16). In "The Manner of Her Will," she again speaks of the infection of figurative decapitation personified in the male figure of London (93-96); people try to cut away or wash away (123) the disease, the "drug" (126) or drudgery of domination in the poem, but it does not remedy the situation. Even the air is contagious in London (124). Decapitation is a suffocation, and Whitney discusses this through a description of the forces at work in London. Cary's Mariam "looses" her breath in the last act of *The Tragedy of Mariam* so that she no longer has to breathe in the oppressive forces in her life. London, the unfaithful suitor in Whitney's poetry, consumes women of the gentry and the women are left poorer for it (133-5).

Figurative decapitation of women is discussed at the outset of the preamble to "The Manner of Her Will" called "A Communication Which the Author had to London Before She Made her Will":

> Wherefore small cause there is that I
> Should grieve from thee to go;
> But many women, foolishly
> Like me and other mo,
> Do such a fixed fancy set
> On those which least deserve,
> That long it is ere wit we get
> Away from them to swerve. (5-12)

Women are loyal and giving to their lovers even when the lovers do not deserve such treatment; women are slow to discover that their love is misplaced. Early modern English conduct manuals encouraged women to be silent in public, and as Paul Marquis explains, this was especially true concerning speaking out against male abuse (315). Whitney meticulously presents her narrator as the epitome of feminine virtues "to escape the Ovidian victim/loquacious whore double bind," as Krontiris explains (35). Whitney depicts London as a domineering male jailer. London is a prison from which the narrator wishes to depart. From line 25 to near the end of "The Manner of Her Will" Whitney describes in detail the structures or buildings that comprise London, representing the government and religious hierarchies that she wants to leave behind. These hierarchies are the source of female figurative decapitation. The narrator explains that she was "bred" (26) among these structures, implying that she was not born of them. Societal rules have dictated the life of the narrator of the poem, but her birth is not figured by these hierarchies.

The different aspects of London that imprison the Early Modern Englishwoman are analyzed in Whitney's "The Manner of Her Will." The "stocks" was a place of public imprisonment and humiliation where women who were judged too brazen with their tongue were often bridled and displayed in the heart of the city at the site of the marketplace, as expounded upon by Lynda Boose and Christoph Hinckeldey.[9] "Eloquence in a woman [was] often associated with aggression or sexual deviancy. A woman's tongue was popularly represented as her phallic weapon," as Kim Walker indicates (11). This display of "deviants" in the center of the marketplace in

---

[9] Lynda E. Boose and Christophe Hinckeldey have written works that graphically illustrate the torture of Early Modern women who would not keep quiet. Boose's article contains pictures of metallic "scold's bridles" that were used to mussel outspoken women in Early Modern England (Figs. 6-8). Hinckeldey's book contains a picture of a town square with bridled women on display similar to the marketplace that Whitney describes in "The Manner of Her Will" (Fig. 2B).

Whitney's poem is connected to male ownership of women as possessions or trophies to be adorned, displayed, and handed from man to man. She ridicules women's vanity that enables their own oppression (65-68). The boy the narrator has "left" by the stocks "will ask you what you lack" (68). In a patriarchal society, women are considered to lack everything and men provide what women need. To subvert the label of female lacking, the poem takes stock or "store" of London, apprises the worth of London, and finds London wanting. This is particularly apparent in the section of the poem about Ludgate: the narrator wills "nothing" to Ludgate (176), a prison for debtors and bankrupts who were often from the lower classes. Women in Early Modern English patriarchy are debtors of a different kind: they lack credit or value. The narrator is leaving London because the narrator is in debt. This debt is related to her station in life, because she must find employment, but her debt is also the devalued state of women in her society. Therefore, the narrator is leaving London because she refuses to choke down figurative decapitation, the devaluing of self simply because she is female. "I feel myself so weak / That none me credit dare" (190-01). The narrator also wills "bankrupts" (192), debtors but also nothingness, to the creditors who put people of her station in life in prison.

Line 49 refers to "Cheap" or Cheapside in London where there are many jewelers, goldsmiths (1) who sell plate "of silver and of gold" trim (55). However, the word *cheap* also refers to the futility or worthlessness of male hoarding and containment of things and people: "In Cheap, of them they store shall find" (49). The wares of the jewelers and goldsmiths "satisfy your mind" meaning London as well as "ladies meet" (52), but the produce of "Cheap" does not satisfy the "will" of the narrator as a representative of the common woman in her society. "And in oblivion bury me / And never more me name" (267-68). The dead are rid of "this vale so vile" (274). Burial "ceremonies" are "lost" (269-72) on those who are devalued by society.

Near the end of the poem, one hundred lines are devoted to describing the structural buildings that are real-life prisons in London, the figure of the Early Modern English patriarchy: the Counter (141), the Hole (147), Newgate (149), the Fleet (165), Ludgate (176), Bridewell (229), a woman's prison, Smithfield (217) where women accused of witchcraft or religious heresy were burned at the stake, and Bedlam (225) where the insane were kept. The prisons are "heaped" with the "infection" (151) of the city. Justice (149-50) cannot cure the disease and even honest men (143) are caught up in the malaise. Whitney spends so much time discussing these prisons and their cruelties that there is obviously some underlying meaning. The poet wants the reader to witness what offenses an unscrupulous suitor can inflict; life with him is like being in the worst of prisons in London.

Also, the society Whitney lived in spent much money on containment of those, debtors, heretics, the insane, who were deemed out of control, bringing chaos or disharmony to order. Women were defined in this same manner: lacking control, heretical, disorderly, and in need of containment: "And though I nothing named have / To bury me withal, / Consider that above the ground / Annoyance be I shall" (261-64). Like the people in Bedlam, women's sexuality was considered to be disruptive, "out of tune" (228) with the order and economy of the hierarchy. In this section of the poem, the poet questions the "sanity" of Early Modern English patriarchy.

The Early Modern English patriarchy also regulated and repressed male/female relationships, as Martin observes; women could not openly mourn a man if he was not her husband or family relation (304). "But woe is me, I live in pinching pain, / No wight doth know what sorrow I sustain" (54). This is a line from the elegy "The Lamentation of a Gentlewoman upon the Death of her Late-deceased Friend, William Gruffith, Gentleman" (1578) in which the narrator celebrates the life of a dear friend and lover by comparing their relationship to famous legendary couples like Admetus and Alcestis.

Specifically, the narrator of the poem is "pained" by the restrictions put on women. Life for women in her situation is full of "woes" (59).

The power over life and death is connected to birthing, to the maternal body (55-58). Later, the narrator explains that death is female: "And when that death is come to pay her due" (79). English men are like Narcissus, in love with their own reflection, and they use women to mirror this image (108). The narrator pictures her beloved, Gruffith, reborn and transformed into a flower as was Narcissus, "Which flower out of my hand will never pass, / But in my heart shall have a sticking place" (113-4). Thus, her heart, like the mind and will of the narrator in "The Manner of Her Will," are steadfast, determined that the woman writer's art is to give birth to a new world for men and women. Also, love is related to the natural world.

However, Whitney's narrator realizes she is dreaming: "But woe is me, my wishes are in vain; / Adieu delight, come crooked cursed care! / To bluntish blocks I see I do complain, / And reap but only sorrow for my share" (115-18). The narrator bids *adieu* to a new world order, to female *jouissance,* and to a merging of discourse because the men she deals with are like "bluntish blocks." Female will or delight is "blunted" by the cares that the real world inflicts on women: "And as I can, I will abide the rest" (124). Women's lives in a patriarchal society are about living with loss; however, the flame of the passion for writing and for a different world for men and women lives on for the narrator in secret: "For as I am, a lover will I die" (132). The narrator must keep her identity secret for fear of societal contempt; women writers must keep their anonymity as well (126). The will to court "Lady Fame" so that she will "spread my praise" (86) but also the fear of societal backlash (129) are constant companions for the woman writer. Women like Whitney and Cary are always in this *entredeux* position, always disruptive because they are at once outside and inside the system. Laurie Ellinghausen concurs with this interpretation of Whitney's text, observing that "Whitney's relationship to her literary labor suggests that a notion of professional authorship could also be formulated by deploying cultural discourses and locating oneself in the spaces in between" (2).

Whitney colors her forbidden desire for writing, "a web of black" in her heart (24), as a poem about the forbidden desire for Gruffith. The narrator frames the web (24) indicating that women are forced to hide or contain their will to *disgorge*, to outpour generosity and loss through text. At the outset of "The Lamentation of a Gentlewoman" the narrator indicates that women are not supposed to write nor call upon the Muses for inspiration. Women are supposed to suppress these desires even though they are a natural part of a woman's embrace of loss as a part of birthing. This poem is dedicated to teaching women about the loss, inability and expression, of disgorgement, camouflaged as eliciting their help in mourning:

> You ladies all, that pass not for no pain,
> But have your lovers lodged in your laps,
> I crave your aids to help me mourn amain;
> Perhaps yourselves shall feel such careful claps,
> Which God forbid that any lady taste,
> Who shall by me but only learn to waste. (25-30)

Women are trained by society to represent lack. Whitney does not want women to absorb this repression from her writing but instead to use their marginalization to express text. Writing the elegy is connected to women's sexuality (26) just as the poet connects writing her will to sexuality at the end of "The Manner of Her Will." The "fashion of her passion" is the outpouring of text.

Disgorgement

> She doesn't try to 'recover her expenses.' She is able not to return to herself, never settling down, pouring out, going everywhere to the other [. . .] Her libido is cosmic, just as her unconscious is worldwide: her writing also can only go on and on. (Cixous, *The Newly Born Woman* 87)

To create an outpouring of text, a writing that can "go on and on" explicating and opposing the woman's position in Early Modern England, Whitney versifies Sir Hugh Plat's book *Flowers of Philosophy* published in 1572. These verses make up Whitney's book *A Sweet Nosegay or Pleasant Poesy* published in 1573 (Martin 279-80). *A Sweet Nosegay* includes the following poems: "To her Brother Geoffrey Whitney," "To her Brother Brooke Whitney," "An Order Prescribed by Isabella Whitney," "To her Sister Mistress Anne Baron," "A Communication" and "The Manner of Her Will." "To her Sister Mistress Anne Baron," similar to Whitney's other poems, was addressed to family members; the narrator attempts to salve her loneliness by cementing the emotional bond with her brother's family, wishing they may have happiness, health, success, and longevity Plat's book is a collection of neo-Senecan moral precepts. Whitney speaks of "borrowing" flowers from Plat's garden and urges other women to do the same in *A Sweet Nosegay*. She is advising women to translate the female body's text into male language. She is also deconstructing linguistic conventions established in Plat's book. The opening lines of *A Sweet Nosegay* are an apology for spending time reading and writing, but her excuse is that idle hands are the devil's workshop. Whitney establishes her motive for writing because as a good Christian woman she should keep busy. Therefore, the author uses her marginalization in the English patriarchy to her advantage in her writing.

Whitney uses her marginalized position in other ways in her writing as well. "Epistle to the Reader" explains the purpose of writing the collection of poems called *A Sweet Nosegay*; each of her poems also contains a short preamble near the opening of the lyric which serves as a structural frame for the piece, explicating the narrator's discursive reasoning. The author's so-called *mental depression* or illness, one of her reasons for writing explained in the "Epistle to the Reader," may be a pose, because women were thought by Early Modern English society to be "hysteric." She is justifying her authorship by saying that depression is "natural" in a woman, using disenfranchisement as an excuse to outpour text. Whitney uses the ruse of a "hysteric's" reaction to apologize to the men in Early Modern English society for her writing; after all, she is "only" a woman. The poet is being sarcastic here, and her humor is an important part of her writing technique. Her *Copy of a Letter* and *A Sweet Nosegay* use camouflaged sardonic humor to comment on social conditions of her time particularly the state of affairs for women of the gentry. I disagree with Krontiris, who reads the poem at face value, that Whitney really was depressed. Although, as Martin points out, Whitney was indeed physically ill for a period of time in her life (280), she was also an expert at using social norms to justify her non-conventional behavior.

In very specific ways, the author narrates the female body's text. The poem "An Order Prescribed by Isabella Whitney" is just one of many of her poems that uses her own name in the title. In this way, the poet creates a narrative voice that appears to be her own, as if her readership is privy to her private correspondence. Yet, as a woman of the gentry who is a published writer, the poet can simultaneously subvert and merge with the narrative voice. In stanza 7 of "To her Sister Mistress Anne Baron," the poet's narrator reveals that "My books and pens I will apply" (42). She wields power over the pen(is) and applies it to the page rather than being inscribed by men. Housewives, like the narrator's sister-in-law Anne Baron, do not have the time to write (37-42). "Good sister so I you commend / To him that made us all, / I know you housewifery intend, / Though I to writing fall" (31-34). Patricia Phillippy bases her discussion of Whitney's poetry on the precept that Whitney defends her role as writer as part of the proper art and duties of "housewifery" (439), but I disagree. Although writing appears to be paralleled with housewifery in lines 33 and 34 of "To her Sister" the connecting word is not "and." The word *though* redirects the reader to another meaning. Writing inoculates the narrator from being placed in a position of subservience to men. Whitney only serves "him that made us all."

Both "The Manner of Her Will" and "The Lamentation of a Gentlewoman" are poems about death. In the latter, Whitney uses the dead body of Gruffith as a springboard to talk about her own passion for writing. In both poems, the use of a dead body's text generates a subversion of literary practices and an outpouring of feelings from the author. Shakespeare and Cary use the dead bodies of Lavinia and Mariam for the same purpose. London is described in "The Manner of Her Will" as the heart of life. Leaving London is a kind of death, but at the same time the narrator sees her leaving as a rebirth. Therefore, she casts aside imprisoning devices of male and aristocratic society, leaving them to various parts of the city, and returns instead to the power of the feminine body, explained in the last section of the poem.

The poem takes stock or "store" of London and its citizenry. In "The Manner of Her Will" and "The Lamentation of a Gentlewoman" a textual loss is the main focus: "In lieu of love, alas, This loss I find" ("The Lamentation of a Gentlewoman" 16). "The latter text is dedicated to a loss, the loss of Gruffith. In "The Lamentation of a Gentlewoman" Whitney writes that "wit wants to will" (11), that feminine "will" is a kind of *jouissance* and is privileged over male jurisdiction, male "wit" or reason, in Early Modern English society. The elegiac form is a camouflage for the true intent of the poem; the poem's intent is to profess Whitney's passion for writing, her commitment to textual disgorgement. She achieves her disgorgement of female text through undermining and also merging with the established literary practices of male society.

Subversion of Language

> Women [. . .] take pleasure in jumbling the order of space, in disorienting it, in changing around the furniture, dislocating things and values, breaking them all up, emptying structures, and turning propriety upside down. (Cixous, "Laugh" 887)

As Ana Kothe explains, Whitney's "subversion [of] a male hegemonic literary order" (16) is exemplified in her verse. Indeed, Whitney's writing, her fragmentation of "structures" and "values," is an intentional maze of voices, hiding behind the employment of male language and patriarchal social dictates, in an attempt to free herself of figurative decapitation and release her voice from containment. The poet's maze of words in her poetry subverts accepted linguistic practices in Early Modern England. She achieves a subversion of male language by playing with phrasing. For example, her use of first person "we" is intentionally ambiguous in her poetry; "we" might include women or men or both, giving Whitney a bisexual narrative position. Therefore, she manipulates her female personae to create the desired impact on her audience, much as Cary does through the use of her female characters in *The Tragedy of Mariam.*

Whitney worked closely with Richard Jones, publisher of her works, and was aware of popular trends in authorship. "Publication was problematic for male writers; for women, the 'stigma of print' was intensified," as Walker argues (22). A complex problem requires a complicated strategy to circumvent it. Whitney had an intricate solution to her authorial problem. What she is not saying is as important as what she is saying.

Copy of a Letter is written as an Ovidian lament in verse epistle and ballad form. This poem "is the closest Whitney comes to expressing a feminist consciousness: seeing women as an oppressed and persecuted group," as Krontiris indicates (38). The Ovidian discourse presented in the pamphlet wars, namely Joseph Swetnam's *The Arraignment of Lewd, Idle, Forward, and Unconstant women* (1615), discusses unfaithful women, reflecting upon and quoting sections of Ovid's *Metamorphoses.* Instead, her poetry from thirty years earlier, particularly "An Order Prescribed by Isabella Whitney," "The Manner of Her Will," and *Copy of a Letter* takes unfaithful men to task. She wants to illustrate how Ovid's writings, as Krontiris demonstrates, "disclose the history of the discourse that teaches men how to be deceptive" (37). This is also apparent in Whitney's "The Admonition by the Auctor," a literary sequel to *Copy of a Letter* where the author combines as she does in *Copy of a Letter* classical allusion and gender discourse, but in "The Admonition," she demonstrates solidarity with other women instead of addressing men and she attacks male poets instead of classical male heroes. In "The Admonition," the narrator refers directly to Ovid's *Ars amatoria:*

> Ovid, within his Arte of love,
> Doth teach them [men] this same knacke
> To wet their hand and touch their eies:
> So oft as tears they lacke."[10]

This poem is focused on legendary women who were deceived by men from Ovid's *Metamorphoses.*

Whitney understands female figurative decapitation, and her approach is wily. She realizes, as Cary inscribed in her daughter's wedding ring, that as long as a woman embodies the motto of "be and seem," to appear to be virtuous in all respects, she can manipulate her position, (Fischer 289). Whitney inscribes the notions of the ideal woman in *Copy of a Letter*; the female waits patiently for the lover to decide whom he will take as his wife. "Wed whom you list, I am content, / your refuse for to be" (83-84). The woman is "content" to be treated as property. However, the narrator's "virtuous woman" testimony in *Copy of a Letter* is a cover for the poet's real purpose, which is to critique the double standard applied to faithless men versus the brand of the female temptress on women in Early Modern England. Men may be untrue to women, but the ideal woman is expected to wait patiently for her lover's return and for her lover to decide whom he will wed. The woman is depicted in her poetry as

---

[10] I am quoting text from Whitney's poem "The Admonition," reprinted on p. 49 in Ann Rosalind Jones's *The Currency of Eros: Women's Love Lyric in Europe, 1540-1620.*

"content" to be treated as property. Women were supposed to be silent concerning male abuse, but whether you are an Early Modern, modern or postmodern woman, I don't think it's possible to miss the sarcasm in lines 83-84. Her cautionary advice to women concerning betrayal in *Copy of a Letter* is used to conceal Whitney's own betrayal of social customs.

Sweetness in speech was considered a "restrained alternative to silence" for women in the Tudor period, as Walker indicates (13). However, Whitney is so sweet in all of her poetry, she's diabetic; her "virtuous woman" testimony is a cover for her real purpose, which is to critique society's expectations about women. *Copy of a Letter* alludes to many unfaithful men from classical literature (Aeneas, Theseus, Jason, Paris) as examples of male betrayal of trusting women. The author patterns *Copy of a Letter* after Ovid's *Heroides*, an amatory verse epistle, as Jones professes, and its diatribe concerning faithless male lovers and the women who try to reclaim the men who have abandoned them ("Writing to Live" 43). The undercurrent of criticism in Whitney's poetics is apparent:

> Now may you heare how falseness is
> > made manyfest in time:
> Although they that comit the same,
> > think it a veniall crime.
> For they, for their unfaithfulness,
> > did get perpetuall fame:
> Fame? wherefore dyd I terme it so?
> > I should have cald it shame. (65-72)

Disgorgement is textual manipulation that offsets a patriarchy's textual inscription of a woman's character, behavior, actions, and place in the societal hierarchy or order. Puns or word play are this sort of textual manipulation in Whitney's "The Manner of Her Will" which contains a series of puns, starting with the title itself, that cues the reader to look for subtext throughout the poem. The title of

Whitney's "Will" alone is an array of word play. A woman's "manner" might be her custom, fashion, method, style, behavior, bearing, or a display or depiction of behavior. It also could be a play on words or homonym for "manor," the housing or receptacle of the female body's text. The "fashion" of much of Whitney's writing is that of the instruction book, a popular type of writing in the Early Modern period. *A Sweet Nosegay*, of which "The Manner of Her Will" is the final section, is a "middle-class conduct book" in verse form, as Krontiris describes it (39). The narrator's instruction in Whitney's poem reveals the "behavior" or "bearing" of a woman of the gentry in Early Modern England.

They were doubly marginalized; the women of the gentry were subservient to all and must be careful to exhibit the female virtues of submission, passivity, chastity, and silence lest they be punished severely. Therefore, their behavior would not include "will" of any kind. Yet, the speaker in Whitney's "Will" does indeed have a will of her own. A woman's "will" could be interpreted as her determination, desire, passion, gift, choice, or intent. Therefore, the poet's "Will," a legally rendered document, has the underlying meaning of also being a discourse that illustrates the fashion of female passion or *jouissance*. A woman's will, especially a woman of the gentry, would disturb the natural order of patriarchal expectations for female manner. In addition, since an unmarried woman of the gentry in the Early Modern period like Whitney would have nothing of value to will to anyone upon her death, and since this woman would have no Will and no will of her own in a society where everything of value is possessed by the patriarchy, the reader must assume the text of the "Will" is really about something else. The poet transforms female nothingness into somethingness through the outpouring of text, since, as Wendy Wall indicates, Whitney's writing is the only real possession she has (75). As an unmarried and childless woman, she has given birth to nothing else.

In the introduction to the "Will" entitled "A Communication Which the Author had to London Before She Made her Will," the narrator's first two lines are: "The time is come, I must depart, / From thee, ah famous city." Time figures prominently in this poem so it is not surprising that the word appears in the very first line. Time in this poem is related to the subversive nature of the discourse; time is reiterated to punctuate the temporal disturbance of the poem. The word *depart* is used again in the title to the body of the "Will" itself, called "The Manner of Her Will, and What She Left to London and to all Those in it, at her Departing." "Depart" can refer to the narrator leaving London in either a physical or spiritual sense, looking for living arrangements in another town or dying and leaving the world of the living. "Depart" can also mean to separate, to break, to fragment, just as disgorgement of the female body's text is defined as giving a "signal to depart," making departure from the masculine economy a gift (Cixous "Castration" 175). Therefore, Whitney's whole poem is set up from the start to subvert meaning. "I never yet, to rue my smart, / Did find that thou hadst pity" ("A Communication" 3-4). The narrator is "smarting" because although she displays her generosity throughout her "Will," London, depicted as a fickle lover in the preamble and in the "Will" itself, has no pity on her to heal her humiliation. The narrator is also "smart"; she has never yet rued her intuitive abilities despite men's censure of women's intellect. The poet inverts Petrarchan discourse where the male lover cannot tear himself away from his beloved even though she may be unfaithful to him, and in Whitney's version and inversion, the jilted female actually does "depart" from her "unconstant lover." "She is outside the city, at the edge of the city,"as Cixous says in another context, and "the city is man" ("Castration" 170).

The "Will" opens with language constructed to imitate a real will, hiding behind religious pretext as a means to express text. Her poetic "Will" has the flavor of Margaret Hoby's real life will and testament. Hoby left the bulk of her estate to her husband's heirs since she had none, and Whitney, with a flare of wit, wills her "estate" to the London populace, as Lena Orlin articulates (255). However, Whitney's opening phrase to her will reverses the wording common to wills written in Early Modern England:

> I whole in body and in mind,
>   But very weak in purse,
> Do make and write my testament
>   For fear it will be worse.
> And first I wholly do commend
>   My soul and body eke
> To God the Father and the Son,
>   So long as I can speak. (1-8)

Compare this verse to the opening lines of her brother, Geoffrey Whitney's will: "I Geoffrey Whitney of Ryle's Green in the County of Cheshire, gentleman, being sick in body but of sound and perfect memory, thanks be to God, therefore make and set down with my own hand this my last will and testament."[11]

Whitney's entire poem is designed to subvert a document of discourse from the patriarchal system that orders society by passing on possessions from one man to the next. "I whole in body and in mind" (1) – this line imitates the actual language of a real-life "Will," but also subverts figurative decapitation because the narrator is "whole in body and in mind." The line also undermines the power of the Petrarchan blazon that anatomizes and objectifies women as mere body parts. She is not anatomized but "whole." The author also reverses the order of the standard "Will" in Western societies, "being of sound mind and body." Her brother, Geoffrey, emphasized the importance of his "sound and perfect memory" in his "Will." In Early Modern English patriarchy, reason is privileged over the text of the

---

[11] Quotations from Geoffrey Whitney will are from Randall Martin's *Women Writers in Renaissance England* (290).

body, but in Whitney's poem, the body comes first, is of most importance. God's speech created the world in Genesis, and the narrator's speech re-creates her body to be inscribed not by men's will, but by God's (5-8).

In fact, she reveals the true purpose of the poem in these lines: "And though I nothing named have / To bury me withal, / Consider that above the ground / Annoyance be I shall" (261-64). Her use of the word *annoyance* here is another display of *jouissance*. Having no husband, no children, and at the time of the "Will," no "virtuous lady" to work for as a servant, the narrator must find a different way to put her body to good use. A dead body is an absent presence, the state of all living women in the patriarchy who must affect a stoic persona. Representing the female speaker in the "Will" as this absent presence places the writer in a non-threatening pose. The speaker's "dead body" is a ruse used to camouflage the voice of the author; with the author's voice "dead," the poem attempts to stand apart from the author's biases to reveal an objective picture of the London scene. It is apparent that Whitney is using the fictionalized dead body of the speaker of the poem as the catalyst for a text that is not a "Will" in the common legal definition, but instead a discourse that deconstructs the powers of the male body, as a unit and as a group, and *disgorges* the female body's text, as a unit and as a group, in a new light. In other words, the female "body" is not as absent, as dead, as the patriarchy would like the world to believe. Instead, the manner of the female "will" is presented in the poem as a powerful entity.

There are precedents for many of Whitney's writing techniques, including the idea of personifying London as the Early Modern male. The Renaissance theory of one depicted as many or many depicted as one was common in European literature and art, according to Edgar Wind (115); the artistic renderings of personified cities or countries (man as microcosm of a larger macrocosm) during the Tudor period include John Donne's elegy XIX and the engraving "America" by Italian artist Giovanni della Strada (Waddington 289). Authorial word play with wills, leaving parts of one's life to others or to abstract concepts was also a literary convention of Whitney's time period; John Ford uses this convention with dramatic effect in *The Broken Heart* where Penthea wills her "jewels" to Calantha. Penthea gives her youth to virgin-wives, her fame to memory and truth, and her brother to Calantha (3.5.60). Moreover, writers of the Early Modern period had an admiration for the rhetorical accomplishments of *imitatio* and *copia* (McGrath 283).

It is therefore not unusual that Whitney's works resonate with the Renaissance stylings of the Petrarchan blazon, the conduct book, the verse epistle, the pamphlet wars exemplified in the writings of "Jane Anger," and literature of private life. The blazon is constructed to anatomize the beloved's body, a fetishizing of the speaker's desires; in the blazon, the speaker's love in unrequited. A female writer in Early Modern England reversing the gender of the blazon was not innovative; other women writers in England during this time period had played with this idea in their poetry, Lady Mary Wroth's sonnet sequence *Pamphilia to Amphilanthus* being a good example. Inverting the discourse of Ovid and Jean de Meun concerning the masculine preoccupation with female unchastity, reverse blazon*s* written by English Renaissance women warn women about fickle male lovers. The reverse blazon did not idealize men as Petrarch's poetry idealized women; on the contrary, Whitney and Wroth criticized men's fickle nature as lovers and at the same time affirmed the positive qualities of devotion and loyalty that virtuous women embodied.

What *is* distinctive about Whitney's "Will" is that her inverted blazon reflects the female body in terms of the gentry rather than the aristocracy, a philosophy that permeates all of her writings. In addition, her "Will" is a far more elaborate criticism of the English patriarchy, inscribed in her poem as the London landscape. London is separated into its different geographical sections in Whitney's poem and the glories of each section are venerated. London is displayed as an object of obsessive reverence and irrational devotion since the speaker cannot cease being generous towards the town despite the town's indifference to the speaker, and the speaker indicates London's horrors without losing the speaker's loyalty.

The blazon also contains flattery and complaints. For example, the word "store" is used numerous times in the poem. The first half of the poem demonstrates how the male world puts great store in displaying "store" as a symbol of its munificence. Personified as a male lover, London appears on the surface to be the kind of suitor every young woman, in any time period would dream of – healthy, hospitable, and charitable. However, abundance and treasury are the outpourings of the female body, not the male body, for Whitney; the word 'store' is fool's gold and used sarcastically throughout the poem to contrast female philanthropy with the stinginess of spirit, affection, and prosperity the English patriarchy actually has for mankind and womankind. London is the kind of smooth-talking, shallow suitor honest, moral women should avoid. For in the second half of the poem, the pretty picture of fruitful London life is undercut by a litany of negligences perpetrated on London's "lovers" or the populace of the town by their "generous" benefactor. These negligences are the blazon's complaints concerning the lover.

London in Whitney's "Will" is originally characterized as bountiful. At the beginning of the "Will," London is teeming with food (33), drink (35), linen (43), silk (47), jewelry (51), plate (53), clothing (57), books (241), schools (247), churches (27); Whitney's "Will" provides for an even greater stock of all finery for the London populace (32). At the same time, however, London houses many sick people (95), thieves (97), prostitutes (120), starving writers, publishers (195), and actors (251), lonely women (201), and the blind and lame (223). London's populace gathers to watch executions of condemned prisoners (160) and witches and heretics (217) as well as the people who are committed to Bedlam, the lunatic asylum, for sport (225). London is characterized in "A Communication . . .l" as unpitying (4) and undeserving of loyalty (9). Whitney's London is not "of woman born" (4.1.80) to borrow a line from Shakespeare's *Macbeth*; Whitney's London is produced by patriarchal institutions of order and structure. London is not a creator as women are through childbirth and through the production of female discourse.

The treasury that women possess is everything that London is not: women are depicted as feeling, giving, and understanding in the poem. The speaker reveals in the "Will" that she is humble (7), reverent (10), joyful (14), trusting (19), generous even with those who oppress her ("A Communication" 31; "The Manner of Her Will" 89 and 275), astute (100), comforting (75), honest (132), meticulous (255), modest (266), thrifty (272), loving even with those who have been cruel to her ("A Communication" 29; "The Manner of Her Will" 278 and 312), kind (283), protective (306), and encouraging (308). The women of London in the "Will" are depicted as courteous (208), innocent and proper (117), happy and quiet (285).

Part of the poet's complaint against London is to contrast it with the treasury of female text. London is depicted, especially at the end of the poem, as a destroyer of lives. London is stingy ("A Communication" 24); for all of London's "store," "he" oppresses the less-fortunate. The "Will" reveals the debilitating effects of poverty (105), filth (124), horrific prisons for debtors (137) and other felons (150), and excruciating torture for petty offenders (154).

The complaints about London in Whitney's blazon outweigh the flattery. London is full of the "dulled minds" (114) of the male body. Everything is a commodity in the patriarchal structure; men keep in order to sell in a closed system of reciprocity.

> If they that keep what I you leave
> Ask money when they sell It
> At Mint there is such store it is
> Unpossible to tell it. (109-12)

Therefore everything in the male economy, including sex and reason, is linked to marketability and commodification. The desires of London

(275-76) are the items listed in the poem "The Manner of Her Will" which the author compares to the desires of the narrator. "They oft shall seek for proper girls / [. . .] That needs compels or lucre lures / To satisfy their minds" (117-20). Male desire is compared and merged with female *jouissance* in the poem.

In line 31, the London populace "craveth cost." London must "keep" or take care of its people. Whitney refers in this line to the male economy that is afraid of loss and craves balance in life's account book of give and take. The female economy is the true "store," one that "craveth cost" also, but in contrast, it desires loss. It gives without return. It gives "more" (32) and imbalances or subverts the order of the patriarchal system. "Such store" (59) is reiterated many times in this poem. She uses the word to delineate the male economy of containing, ordering, and hoarding versus the female economy of giving from her "store." Using the word in both ways creates a link between men and women, in the way they suppress and lose their "store." The word becomes connected to the oppression of the female body by men due to fear of loss.

Whitney's poem as blazon anatomizes London, the narrator's male lover, just as courtier poets imitated Petrarch's blazon to characterize women of their time period. The speaker directly addresses London as a person more than once ("A Communication" 21, 35; "The Manner of Her Will" 253, 289); London is also stipulated as the executor of the speaker's "Will" (277). However, the Petrarchan blazon is used to *idealize* women. Whitney's blazon characterizes her *man* as corrupt, selfish, and cruel. The speaker in the poem rebukes London:

> And now hath time me put in mind
>   Of thy great cruelness,
> That never once a help would find
>   To ease me in distress.
> Thou never yet wouldst credit give
>   To board me for a year,

> Nor with apparel me relieve
>> Except thou payed were.
> No, no, thou never didst me good
>> Nor ever wilt, I know. ("A Communication" 17-26)

In "The Lamentation of a Gentlewoman," the author once again subverts the Petrarchan blazon by anatomizing Gruffith through the use of colors of clothing rather than body parts (13-18). She uses the modesty topos in most of her poems; many examples appear in "The Lamentation of a Gentlewoman." "My wits be weak an epitaph to write" (31), "My phrase doth serve but rudely to recite" (33), "Then had it been that I, poor silly dame, / Had had no need to blot this scratched scroll" (49-50), "Wherefore I do attempt so much the more / By this good hope to show my slender art" (67-68), and "But I, poor I, as I have said before, / Do wail to want Minerva's learned lore" (95-96). However, the author undermines her professions of inability to compose well by continuing to write, in this case sixteen more sestets. This balance of modesty and disgorgement *speaks* to the figurative decapitation of women in male-governed societies who must maintain a façade of humility at all costs. The narrator compares her meager poetic gifts with Gruffith's male friends who were writers (37-44). Whitney does not praise these writers and their "rhyme rough" (40).

Furthermore, through repetition, the modesty topos loses its intent of muting the words of a "weak woman." The repetition sounds like sarcasm; the author does not really believe that her writing and publishing are inappropriate activities for a woman of her class. The narrator asks her "mournful muse, good ladies" to give "worth" to her writing (73). The passion for writing is "recorded" within the breast of a woman (76), "and there is lodged forever to remain" (77); she has dared to "publish forth" her poetry (75).

> So live I shall, when death hath spit her spite,
> And Lady Fame will spread my praise, I know,
> And Cupid's knights will never cease to write

And cause my name through Europe for to flow:
And they that know what Cupid can prevail,
Will bless the ship that floats with such a sail. (85-90)

Through writing, the narrator experiences *jouissance*, a merging of the praise of fame and the place in destiny that a love of writing will create. The narrator explains that if her writing is blessed by goddesses and muses, "By tract of time, great volumes I would fill" (93). Through the lapse of time, Whitney hopes her work will be a part of great volumes and inspire other women writers.

"By help, I hope, these ragged rhyme shall go, / [. . .] and 'scape the chaps of chiding every foe" (97, 99). She writes in the hope to bring the dead back to life, her friend Gruffith as well as the female body at large in Early Modern England; in addition, she reverses female decapitation by inscribing through her poem male life and death.

Though death has shaped his most untimely end,
Yet for his praise my tristive tunes I send,
In hope the gods, who guide the heav'ns above,
His buried corpse alive again will make" (101-04).

Her words are written to "restore" the poem's subject to life (110); thus, language has the power of creation, just as language creates woman in the Early Modern English patriarchal image.

One of the major contrivances Whitney uses is the idea that her art is really artless. In "The Lamentation of a Gentlewoman," the narrator pronounces the theme of artless art, her unworthiness as a woman writer, no less than 11 times (2, 9, 11, 31, 33, 49, 50, 68, 95, 96, 97). This repetition of qualifying her own narration represents one aspect of Whitney's use of subversive textual devices. She also utilizes the conceits of Petrarchan and Ovidian love poetry to express her subversive views on love, sexuality, and mourning (61-66).

Jouissance through Bisexual Discourse

> She excels at marrying oppositions and taking pleasure in this as a single pleasure with several hearths. (Cixous, *Feminine* 209)

It is apparent that Whitney "takes pleasure," as evidenced in her use of humor, in creating a subversive text as well as a bisexual discourse in her poetry. In "Auctor to the Reader," she claims she has had to give up reading works by classic male writers such as Ovid because they "mazed" her "muse" and "bruised" her "brain," as McGrath notes (286). She is being sarcastic since although she often used Ovid's writings as a model for her own, Ovid's works were widely prohibited to female readers, as Phillippy reveals (459). In "The Manner of Her Will," the narrator of the poem speaks of the booksellers at St. Paul's, men like Whitney's publisher. She merges the writing of her poem, a disgorgement of female text, with that of the publishers of male texts.

Writing and publishing is an art that is also connected to nothingness, a futile enterprise, since text is not reality; in a clever turn of phrase, the narrator bequeaths

> To all the bookbinders at St. Paul's,
> Because I like their art,
> They every week shall money have
> When they from books depart. (193-96)

On the surface, the narrator wishes the bookbinders to sell many books, but the phrase also means that the publishers will make money as soon as they depart from selling books. Therefore, the only writing of substance from which the narrator wishes profits to amass is from her own printer (197). Whitney is most probably referring here to Richard Jones, her publisher, who specialized in printing the works of women writers. Her writing is connected to the talents of her male publisher in this passage of the poem.

More importantly, St. Paul's was a male arena, a marketplace where lawyers, merchants, soldiers, and cony catchers gathered. Women were excluded from this public exchange. Also, St. Paul's was a cathedral with a courtyard, a sacred place. The female body was also depicted in male writing, such as the Petrarchan blazon, as a sacred site of discourse. Therefore, St. Paul's as depicted in Whitney's poem serves the dual purpose of a place of merged and subverted discourse. Her poem creates an interchange of discourse between the central discourse, the public discussion of men who were scholars and business associates in St. Paul's square as well as the publications of male writers, and that of a disenfranchised group, women writers. She blends her poem's discussion of faithless men from a woman's viewpoint with the exchange of language at St. Paul's and at the same time undercuts male discourse by discussing St. Paul's in terms of how much money she and her publisher will make on her writing. The commodification of women has merged with female discourse and also has been replaced by a different marketplace of inscription.

To offset the figuratively *decapitating* effects of English patriarchy, the narrator asks the reader to bear "witness" to her "Will" and "will":

Thus have you heard touching my soul
And body, what I mean;
I trust you all will witness bear
I have a steadfast brain. (17-20)

The reader is pulled into the narration, witnessing and connecting with the female writer's mind as the poem unfolds. The reader also witnesses the merging of the narrator's "soul and body" (13-16). The narrator's mind is "steadfast" or determined; it is connected to her steadfast "will." The reader is asked to "witness bear" that women have minds and reason as well as bodies, thus subverting figurative decapitation. The reader as witness to the "Will" and "will" of the narrator is connected here to the other witnesses of the poem: God ("The Manner" 3), time ("A Communication" 1, 13; "The Manner" 323), and "Paper, Pen and Standish" ("The Manner" 321).

The speaker finishes the "Will" by stating that the only "ciphers" to her "great accompt" (Prologue to *Henry V,* line 17) are "Paper, Pen, and Standish" as well as "Time" ("The Manner" 321, 323). These four simple items are the "witnesses" (319) to her "Will" and will. Moreover, these items are the "store" of female outpouring; they are the grand muses, contrasted to the Muses of male writers, which Whitney invokes to assist her in creating her disgorgement. "Time," one of the witnesses to her "Will," is depicted as a woman who is the speaker's friend ("A Communication" 14; "The Manner" 323). Borrowing imagery from Susan Gubar, Evelyn Gajowski, and Janet Adelman, it is my contention that the paper in the "Will" is the symbol of the female as blank page that the Early Modern English patriarchy manipulates, the inkwell represents the female womb that contains the blood of birthing that women use as their ink, and Time is the blessing and curse of life and death that birthing produces. The "Pen(is)" is surrounded by items associated with women in the line of poetry; female outpouring from the "Will" and will has engulfed, swallowed up the power the "Pen(is)" can evoke and has, in effect, temporarily castrated patriarchal power. The intercourse or figurative coitus between the "Pen(is)" and the paper, ink, and Time has created Whitney's *jouissance*, the production of writing.

The "Pen(is)" also represents the convention of the blazon, the use of London as the fickle male lover in her poem, that the poet has subverted to produce her verse. In this way, she creates her own discourse of veiled defiance by manipulating popular writing traditions. Through her "Will" and will, the author has created text out of the blank page the patriarchy makes of women. The word 'will' also connotes the future tense verb; through the imagined legacy of the text of her "Will," the author passes on the real value of the female body's *jouissance* so that future generations of women can perpetuate the process. The function of the female body is to produce life, and life is always a saga. The "Will" tells *his story* or the history of Early Modern London as a means to actually reveal *herstory*.

In "The Lamentation of a Gentlewoman," the author uses various allusions to mythology, including one about Admetus and Alcestis where she parallels her own life to theirs and, as Martin points out, also reverses gender roles by "representing herself as a female Heracles" (309). This is a perfect example of the way in which the author merges her writing with male literary practices, in this case the didactic use of a legendary hero, to camouflage her own textual disgorgement. Typical female stoicism is portrayed in the lines

> Since wailing no way can remedy me,
> To make an end I therefore judge it best,
> And drink up all my sorrow secretly,
> And as I can, I will abide the rest. (121-24)

However, the publication of this poem signifies expression, not containment. Therefore, as Martin indicates, there is always the merging in her poetry of the author's "self-determination and personal expression" with the "submission to social conventions within which she must live" (306). Her poetry always joins the English society's acceptance of male and female stereotypes of identity and demeanor through her writing.

The narrator states "But I, a maid, am forced to use my head" (9) in "The Lamentation of a Gentlewoman." To create poetry, maids must link up with the head, the domain of men. "But as I am, so will I still be bent: / No blasts shall blow my linked love awry" (46-47). The narrator criticizes the "blasts" (47) from the would-be poets or "worldly friends" (43) of Gruffith who try to do him justice. Her love for Gruffith is "linked" or private, not "worldly." It is a woman's place to bend her will to men, but the narrator also suggests that she is "bent" or pledged to her own desires.

Conclusion

> I would define a feminine textual body as a *female libidinal economy* [. . .] a feminine textual body is recognized by the fact that it is always endless, without ending: there's no closure, it doesn't stop, and it's this that very often makes the feminine text difficult to read. (Cixous, "Castration" 174).

Whitney's "The Manner of Her Will" and "The Lamentation of a Gentlewoman" are works that disgorge the "endless" generosity and loss of the "female libidinal economy"; these poems are about giving to others. In addition, her poetic creations do not perpetuate the woman as "blank page"(Gubar 295); she manipulates the unique opportunity through her writing to create an outpouring of the female body, what Cixous defines as the *jouissance* of disgorgement. Whitney's "Will" and "will" reveal the female body as text, not the female body as blank page. Her "Will" does not, as Gubar puts it, illustrate the creation of art by destroying the female body (302). The body as text displays and characterizes the female body in a new way. The female body as text is a discourse that resists; it is an outpouring of expression that subverts the code of stoicism for women in Early Modern England. For Mary Ellen Lamb, emotional suppression is submission, which eventually becomes "self-erasure" (225). Self-erasure is part of the notion of woman as blank page, the very thing Whitney's writing opposes. Her writing takes the privileged place of the male lover or husband who does not exist in her life. The narrator's "Will" and "will" are the poet's disgorgement, because they reveal the author's desire and satisfaction in life through her writing, writing that simultaneously criticizes and merges with male literary practices.

CONCLUSION: THE FEMALE BODY'S TEXT
IN THE TWENTY-FIRST CENTURY

The primary aim of this project is to show how four individual writers voiced women's *jouissance* from their perspectives. This is not to say that all women in Early Modern England felt oppressed or felt a desire to express dissatisfaction with their lives. However, certain conclusions about Early Modern society can be drawn from the scrutiny of the texts discussed in this book. Life for women could be violent and harsh, but women were expected to embrace such conditions stoically. The women of the aristocracy were not always treated better than women of the lower classes. Women's bodies were defined as male property, and women's sexuality was under the jurisdiction of men and used as part of the interplay between men when dealing with the spoils of war or when trying to solidify a place for the man in the political hierarchy. The legitimate claims of the affiliation of a wife and child to a man could be questioned, putting the woman and her child into a precarious domestic situation. Therefore, women lived in fear of being disowned and cast aside. A marketable asset of women in this tenuous situation was a woman's beauty and her ability to give birth to male children. In addition, women did not always give aid to one another. Women were isolated from each other by the laws and customs of male-governed society. It was impossible for women to be united against the oppressive circumstances they lived with.

Although Early Modern English literature could be used as social and political propaganda, it could also be used to reflect and comment upon the life that the authors experienced and the lives of others that the writer viewed from a distance. Female characters in literature had import only in their relationship to male figures of authority in the play. Domestic conflict in Elizabethan drama could be as bloody and pointless as foreign wars. However, there were male authors who revealed in their works that the oppression of women was unconscionable. Women of the aristocracy and of the gentry in the Elizabethan and Jacobean periods in England, women like Cary and Whitney, struggled with censorship, especially the censorship of the female author. They, along with men like Shakespeare, decided to make statements about women in their society through their literary characters and narrators, women who were at times in life-or-death situations where the dead or dying female body had something to communicate.

Cary, Shakespeare, Milton, and Whitney used metaphor to disguise and manifest authorial commentary on their own society by showing how women in past worlds, women like Lavinia in ancient Rome or Mariam in ancient Judea, led muted lives not unlike those of their real-life counterparts in Early Modern England. Being silenced led these female characters to desperate means to communicate the female body's text. Furthermore, women of the gentry in Renaissance England had to be clever, even more clever than women of privilege if they wanted to express themselves. Cary and Whitney were among a handful of women who attempted to emphasize the female characters in a literary work rather than the male characters; notice that Cary's play is not called "The Story of Herod." These women and their writings mark the very early beginnings of what later was named the feminist movement.

The French feminists are often criticized in the contemporary world for an essentialist approach to criticism and for universalizing in their theories the female experience that is far too varied to be generalized; therefore, many contemporary feminists are uncomfortable interrogating the female material body as text. As a result, the influence of the French feminists has been on the wane from the latter part of the twentieth century to the present, as Pamela Banting points out (226). By focusing on the "other" rather than the "mother" and adding plurality to the words "body," "feminism," and "gender," anti-essentialists try to counter linguistic and critical universalism. However, feminists who protest essentialism often end up creating essentialist statements of their own without realizing it. For example, Banting indicates that Toril

Moi's anti-essentialist analysis of Cixous in her book *Sexual/Textual Politics* contains various essentialist errors (227). In addition, the discredit of universalizing constructs does not take into consideration that marginalized groups do have certain characteristics in common. The stigma of essentialism, according to Banting and Naomi Schor, is a form of "excommunication" (226) that discounts and silences all of the work by the French feminists concerning *l'écriture féminine* and the longing for the maternal archaic. I agree with Banting's argument; I believe contemporary criticism should be open to all women's discourses. Therefore, to label any feminist discourse and thereby discount it, is a form of "intellectual terrorism" (226) that I do not want to embrace. I believe all women's voices should be evoked and validated.

In the mid-twentieth century United States classroom, the study of the female characters in Early Modern English plays was subordinated to the study of male characters. A cacophony of *privileged* voices and their agendas is excavated from Early Modern drama and poetry but this emphasis drowns out all other voices. This type of scholarship perpetuates the silencing of women's voices as one of many "othered" groups in Early Modern England. This type of scholarship reveals that our society continued to acknowledge the primacy of the patriarchy rather than the diversity of our civilization. Contemporary advertisements achieve the same affect: they privilege the male gaze. This gives students and viewers of advertisements a skewed vision of the societies women of the seventeenth and twenty-first centuries are part of, that women and all "othered" groups are swallowed up by and exist invisibly inside male systems and structures. It appears as if the Early Modern woman condones her own oppression which was not the case. Therefore, a large part of historical and social erudition is ignored.

The scholarship of feminist critics that began world-wide in the twentieth century to change the reading of literature in classrooms and in criticism must continue. By privileging an examination of those who were not in control, we see a very different picture of Early Modern society, one in which the systems and structures do not seem so omnipotent, one in which those who possessed and managed "othered" groups of people do not look so heroic. The systems and the literature appear more complex and intricate than a one-dimensional perspective of a society's history and culture. This interrogation of a society makes the system seem so much more rich and full than just a cardboard cutout. The implications of encouraging others to interrogate literature in a detailed sense are that the academic community who embraces diversity encourages those students in their classroom who make up a portion of society at large to take a critical look at the perpetuation of patriarchal propaganda. Students will not look at history, at government, at sociology, at advertising, and most importantly, at literature, in the same ways.

Also in this text, I wanted to open out the similarities rather than the differences between the cultures of the United States and England during contemporary and Early Modern time periods, respectively. Too often, we view literature from the past as this far off place with people that have little to do with contemporary life. This concentration on the differences between us walls the reader away from understanding how Early Modern English lives inform our own. Also, there are numerous stereotypes about Early Modern Englishwomen, for example that they were all silent and obedient, that need to be interrogated. The examination of Early Modern English writers should lead us to a greater appreciation of their contribution to what would be termed "feminist" writing in contemporary times and an admiration of the struggle of Early Modern women writers to be heard. There were brave women and men in Early Modern England who wrote about their world through the veiled discourse of another world, as Shakespeare and Cary did. There were and still are progressive women and men who fight for women's rights through the change of societal mores and governmental laws throughout the world. Silenced voices enable the oppression of women everywhere. Knowing the audience is important to successful writing and to social change. In addition, there were women in Early Modern

Europe who were bridled and shamed in the marketplace. There are those who were and are in a position to wield language; George Dugdale's manipulation of the press about the hanging of Elizabeth Caldwell for poisoning her husband in 1603 seems very current and no different than many of the stories that people read in the tabloids today.

Writing is a thermometer, a gauge of figurative decapitation; interrogating a society's writing reveals the manipulation of female sexuality within that culture. Scholars study writing to glean information about the relationships between men and women and between the empowered and disempowered; scholars study writing to see how writing is manipulated to oppress the marginalized or to express the disturbance of the status quo by the disenfranchised. In this project, I wanted to connect the twentieth-century theories of a French feminist to Early Modern English literature to find out what the literature of sixteenth-century England says about the oppression and expression of women. For young American scholars in particular, the literature of centuries long ago written in other countries sometimes seems difficult to embrace.

However, there are palpable threads of commonality between contemporary Americans and Renaissance English men and women that appear in our respective literatures. For one thing, there are young, contemporary American women who believe that we are more emancipated than the women who lived in Early Modern England, and yet all American women are still dealing with the residue of figurative decapitation that is exemplified in sixteenth-century English drama and poetry. Because of the residual effects of patriarchal control of female gender and sexuality, the first and second waves of the feminist movement, the suffragettes campaign for the vote, birth control, the Betty Friedan-generation's quest for equal pay for equal work, and a more open dialogue concerning sexual practices and proclivities were born. The contemporary feminists who are seeking equality, the liberal and socialist feminists, are attempting to create a dialogue with men that is similar to Cixous's concept of a joining or blending of discourse which Cixous calls "bisexual." Cixous does not intend to connote a sexuality that embraces intercourse with both sexes, the common, contemporary use of the word *bisexual*. *Bisexual* is a blending of *l'écriture féminine* and male dependence on written and verbal languages.

The contemporary feminists seeking to emphasize their difference from men and male constructs *disgorge* their text in a way comparable to Cixous's discussion of the disruptive force that comes from the subversion of language by women writers. Part of my project emphasizes the importance of investigating the Early Modern Englishwoman within her culture and as reflected in literature as a tool that informs contemporary feminist theoretical positions and that reveals the commonality between women in the sixteenth and twenty-first centuries. I believe contemporary American, French, and British feminists, among others, are still dealing with issues that were prevalent in the literary endeavors of writers like Cary, Shakespeare, Milton, and Whitney. For example, these writers discussed how language privileged male society and how language produced meaning as well as the ways in which women characters were portrayed in literature. These three authors interrogated *herstory* and revealed how political and social power relationships impacted women's lives. These writers were doing the same work that contemporary feminists are still pursuing. Figurative decapitation and women's propensity to *disgorge* has not dissipated and is not dead simply because scholars find evidence of it in ancient literatures; remnants exist and appear in contemporary social relationships and in contemporary journalism. Contemporary men and women still deal with the vestiges of figurative *decapitating* language; contemporary women writers still fight to *disgorge* their texts. Of course, one of the reasons scholars study Renaissance literature is its facile applicability to modern constructs and lives. This is notable in the adaptation of Shakespeare's plays to modern settings, as in the Baz Luhrman film version of *Romeo and Juliet* or Tim Blake Nelson's *O*.

Female figurative decapitation still exists in contemporary societies; for example, in third world countries, figurative decapitation is pervasive, made manifest through veiling ordinances, arranged marriages, and the practices of clitorectomy, sati, and dowry death. Female decapitation of women in Western cultures today is more subtle but no less noxious: I am speaking of a form of contemporary "literature," of the advertisement. Decapitation advertisements, depicted in television commercials, print ads, and billboards that objectify women by showing women to be all body, are used to silence the voices of contemporary women. Contemporary advertising techniques parallel the suffocating and humiliating effects of Petrarchan and Ovidian discourse by idealizing women or denigrating them and by not embracing the reality of all women. There are feminists who are interested in how female body image is portrayed in United States' advertising in the twenty-first century and how this affects how women "see" themselves.

Contemporary advertising is no different in the way it dispenses propaganda about women's voices and sexuality than the conduct manuals prescribing female behavior and pamphlet wars about the nature of "woman" in Early Modern England. "Within the cult of gender, members are required to weave the continual maintenance of the cult into their daily lives," as Kate Bornstein asserts (103). Corporeality expresses what it is to be female. This was true in Early Modern England and also true today for women in most cultures. The body's text says something about the culture a person lives in. Figurative decapitation says something about how Early Modern English society viewed the female body's text. To *disgorge* text, writers had to overcome the disabling nature of their own society's view of the female body; these writers had to beat the Early Modern English patriarchy at its own game of manipulating the female body's text.

Whitney discussed body image when she spoke about the figuratively *decapitating*, imprisoning effects of women's clothing in

"The Manner of Her Will." Cary interrogated the suppression of women through emphasizing beauty as a trait to be cultivated and manipulated through her character, Mariam. Milton examines Eve's beauty and compares it to his disfigured description of Sin to tease out figuratively decapitating texts about women in Jacobean England. In the twentieth century, John Berger examined this same issue; Berger indicated that women in most contemporary societies worldwide are valued for their beauty and behavior but not for their accomplishments. Women have two selves: the real self and the image that is their constant companion. Women are always surveying themselves and being surveyed. "Men act and women appear," as Berger puts it (47).

I cannot help but note the recent trend towards ultra slimness in Western culture. What does this propensity towards emaciation say about how much equality and freedom has been gained by the women's movements? How much progress have women made toward emancipating their bodies or their sexuality since the days of women like the character Mariam in ancient Judea, or women like the character of Lavinia in ancient Rome, or women like Cary and Whitney from Early Modern England? Today, women in the United States can vote, women can work in jobs gendered as masculine, but women are still surveying their attractiveness according to male standards of desire, just like the female characters in Cary's play. Female self-surveillance enslaves and oppresses. Is ultra thinness a statement of individuality or a step backward, totally embodying the androcentric desire for women to be silent, obedient, chaste, and therefore invisible? I have been wrestling with this dilemma. I see how thinness is a statement of protest towards the common trend of plumpness or fatness; all societies in all cultures view fatness as a sign of prosperity. In contemporary Western societies, we know obesity is unhealthy. However, I keep coming back to a theoretical perspective: repression of indulgence is the basis for stoicism, encouraged as the proper behavior for women by all patriarchies.

Sociologist Sandra Bartky applies Michel Foucault's theory on surveillance or "panopticism" to the female personae in contemporary patriarchies. She discusses Foucault's conclusion that people who are incarcerated constantly deal psychologically with a "third eye." In other words, the belief that someone is watching them from a central position is internalized by prisoners. Bartky's twentieth-century treatise indicates that self-surveillance is an unending prison that women also deal with; women are concerned about their bodies and looks. Women pursue the ideal body image, using makeup and dieting and plastic surgery. Media images surround us with the perfect face and body for a woman; recently, the body image is that of a young woman. The immature, waif-like body is pursued, because it represents the patriarchal ideal woman: submissive, chaste, quiet, obedient.

Bartky says that a "woman's body language speaks eloquently, though silently, of her subordinate status in a hierarchy of gender" (229). Although older forms of oppression die away with female resistance to them, new forms of suppression just take their place. Chastity is not a crucial issue in most Western countries today; instead, the visual image of a woman's body has become the focus of patriarchal constraint, spreading to all classes, not just the aristocracy. Bartky indicates that female "self-surveillance is a form of obedience to patriarchy" (230). Male-governed society wants women to be repressed physically, verbally, sexually, and emotionally. A child's body does not have the sexual subtext or the sexual threat attached to a real woman's sexual body with hips and breasts. Catharine MacKinnon, a contemporary feminist and Marxist theorist, raises the question: "Is women's sexuality its absence?" (182). My gut reaction to all this idealization of thinness as the epitome of beauty is that women absolutely must start embracing heterogeneous body types and promote acceptance of all women if the women's movement(s) hope to be successful in any society and in any era.

Advertisements are one of the most insidious ways in which oppression of women is omnipresent in contemporary cultures. Granted, some advertising critiques society, but most marketing reflects the "market" it targets, just as women writers like Cary and Whitney in Early Modern England shaped their narratives towards what the market would accept. Women are still commodified around the world. Shakespeare, Cary, and Whitney were voicing the position of women in England in their era. The issue of proper behavior for women concerning public versus private speech in Early Modern England is discussed in Cary's closet drama and in Whitney's poetry. They interrogate public and private speech as it relates to public versus private female sexuality, the visibility versus invisibility of the female body's text. The female body's contained text is still an issue in contemporary societies; transgendered individuals, exotic dancers, porn stars, phone sex workers, and prostitutes are today's targets for censure. These "bad girls" in the contemporary U.S. are paralleled with the scolds, shrews, and adulterers of yesteryear. The sexual commodification of women who live in the United States in contemporary times is reflected in twenty-first century advertisement. Non-verbal communication is featured in advertising all the time. The female body's text in the forms of gestures, facial expressions, body posturing and poses, non-verbal cues like clothing and body image are all used to sell products in the United States. What do ads "say" about the subjectivity of women in the United States in the twenty-first century? Isn't there still a double standard; isn't there still stereotyping of the good girl and the bad girl that was in effect repressing women in England in the Elizabethan and Jacobean periods?

Decapitation advertising is one of the worst forms of objectifying women. In these ads, the women have no heads, no identity, no individuality. They are commodities used to sell products, reduced to the Petrarchan blazon of body parts. A case in point is the Levi Strauss hip-hugger jeans ad that aired on television in the United States a few years ago. In the ad, we never see these women's faces; crotch shots are the emphasis of the commercial. Is there not a kind of monstrous female sexuality attached to that Levi-Strauss ad that the patriarchy wants to control and censor? Is this monstrous sexuality any different from that which is portrayed in Shakespeare's Tamora? In what Lavinia's gang raped and mutilated body "says" about the commodification of women? Ironically, the lyric used in the ad is "I'm coming out / I want the world to know / Got to let it show," as if to sound the trumpet of female sexual emancipation, but I think the song masks a more powerful subliminal message. The daughters of Eve who might purchase the Levi-Strauss product represent the attitude from the Early Modern period in England that a wagging tongue connoted a free sexual appetite. Likewise, contemporary women who show their navels are rebellious and outspoken.

This ad reflects a residual form of "bridling" that concerns the female body and how women's clothes in any era are a demarcation of figurative decapitation. The advertisers have made "puppets" of these models and the women who buy the product, just as the men in *Titus Andronicus* try to make a puppet out of Lavinia in the first act of the play by using her as a bartering chip, nullifying the female models' claims of independence and freedom, revealing that female lack still exists in the androcentric society of the United States in the twenty-first century.

Most important of all, the women in the ad are made to appear silly. In this manner, feminism and the feminist movement are ridiculed. This is just one of many ads in the United States that speaks to the issue of monstrous female sexuality which is depicted as castrating and, therefore, must be silenced. An old Virginia Slims cigarette ad professes "You've come a long way, baby," but this is ultimately a disabling United States slogan for women, not fact. It lures women into a false sense that the censure of women no longer exists.

What contemporary feminist criticism has made apparent is that the systems in Early Modern England that figuratively *decapitated* women are still with us but that these systems are not as easily definable and discernable as past criticism might indicate. Silencing is a complex layering of restraints that makes the achievement of disgorgement complicated as well. In addition, figurative decapitation of each woman in Early Modern England had its own specific properties. There is no essential way to silence women or for women to express discourse. The fragmentation or chaos of text that constitutes the disgorgement of the women does not make these women inscrutable but, on the contrary, indicates there is much beneath the surface to investigate.

The female inhabitants of this time period do not fit neatly into the "great chain of being" as stipulated in *The Elizabethan World Picture* by E. M. W. Tillyard, a theory that was once thought to have credibility in critical circles, and women were not merely weak, submissive, and silent as the stereotype of women from this time period would suggest. The subversion of literary constructs implies that the disenfranchised were not helpless and that they used the disgorgement of text to validate their position. Female writers produced distinct texts from one another, and there are varied female voices to be heard in texts written during this time period. One type of voice comes from the female body's text, a viable form of communication that reveals other layers within literature.

The literary canon has been dominated by male writers for centuries; therefore, it is important for contemporary feminist critics to spotlight female writers and characters in publication and in the classroom. Women writers in Early Modern England have been virtually neglected until the past decade or two, and there is a treasury of hidden stories of women waiting to be explored. The voices of these women contribute to *herstory* or the tradition of stories that needs to be recuperated so that contemporary women can understand themselves in relation to their heritage. Understanding a woman's heritage simultaneously enables her voice and gives credence to it. "A woman writing thinks back through her mothers" as Virginia Woolf famously put it (97). Recuperating *herstory*, moreover, enables contemporary students of Early Modern England to obtain a more accurate and complete understanding of the literature and the society of the period formerly known as the

"Renaissance." Education is a powerful tool towards offsetting marketplace propaganda and creating progress for women in the future. These are the things that the female voices in the works of Cary, Shakespeare, Milton, and Whitney say to me.

The main reason I wanted to write about the disgorgement of women writers in England during the sixteenth and seventeenth centuries is that these women speak to contemporary women in all countries about what it is like to be female in a male world. No matter how progressive and enlightened we think we have become, these female voices still have something of import to convey, not only about the past but, more importantly, about our present condition. Textual disgorgement, today and yesterday, offsets the debilitating propaganda of figurative decapitation for women. However, all that I have just said is irrelevant and idealistic, as Annette Kolodny astutely pronounces, as long as women continue to emphasize female voices merely in the fictional world of literature, in the ivory towers of educational institutions, and do nothing to confront and to attempt to solve the problems of real women in today's world. Ultimately, fictional study should facilitate a commitment to eradicate real-life situations of figurative decapitation.

WORKS CITED

Adelman, Janet. *Suffocating Mothers.* New York: Routledge, 1992.

Aebischer, Pascale. *Shakespeare's Violated Bodies: Stage and Screen Performance.* Cambridge: Cambridge University Press, 2004.

Anger, Jane. *The Protection for Women.* London: Richard Jones and Thomas Orwin, 1589.

Banting, Pamela. "The Body as Pictogram: Rethinking Hélène Cixous's *Écriture féminine .*" *Textual Practice* 6 (Summer 1992): 225-46.

Baring, Anne and Jules Cashford. *The Myth of the Goddess: Evolution of an Image.* London: Viking Arkana, 1991

Barry, Peter. *Beginning Theory: An Introduction to Literary and Cultural Theory.* New York: Manchester University Press, 1995.

Bartky, Sandra. "Foucault, Femininity and the Modernisation of Patriarchal Power." In *Women's Studies: Essential Readings.* Ed. Stevi Jackson. New York: New York University, 1993. 227-30.

Beilin, Elaine V. "Elizabeth Cary and *The Tragedie of Mariam.*" *Papers on Language and Literature* 16.1 (Winter 1980): 45-64.

Beilin, Elaine V. *Redeeming Eve: Women Writers of the English Renaissance.* Princeton: Princeton University Press, 1987.

Belsey, Catherine. *The Subject of Tragedy: Identity and Difference in Renaissance Drama.* New York: Methuen and Company, Limited, 1985.

Bennett, Alexandra G. "Female Performativity in *The Tragedy of Mariam.*" *Studies in English Literature 1500-1900* 40.2 (Spring 2000): 293-309.

Berger, John. *Ways of Seeing.* New York: Penguin, 1973.

Boose, Lynda E. "Scolding Brides and Bridling Scolds: Taming the Woman's Unruly Member." In *Materialist Shakespeare.* Ed. Ivo Kamps. New York: Verso, 1995. 239-79.

Bornstein, Kate. *Gender Outlaw.* New York: Vintage, 1995.

Bump, Jerome. "Christina Rossetti and the Pre-Raphaelite Brotherhood." Kent 322-45.

Butler, George F. "Milton's Pandora: Eve, Sin, and the Mythographic Tradition." *Milton Studies* 44 (2005): 153-78.

Butler, Judith. "Subversive Bodily Acts." *Gender Trouble: Feminism and The Subversion of Identity*. New York: Routledge, 1990. 128-41.

Carroll, William C. "The Virgin Not: Language and Sexuality in Shakespeare." In *Shakespeare and Gender: A History*. Ed. Deborah E. Barker and Ivo Kamps. New York: Verso, 1995. 283-301.

Cary, Elizabeth. *The Tragedy of Mariam, the Fair Queen of Jewry with The Lady Falkland; Her Life*. Ed. Margaret W. Ferguson and Barry Weller. Berkeley: University of California Press, 1994.

Catty, Jocelyn. *Writing Rape, Writing Women in Early Modern England: Unbridled Speech*. New York: St. Martin's Press, 1999.

Chambers, A. B. "Three Notes on Eve's Dream in *Paradise Lost*." *Philological Quarterly* 46 (1967): 186-93.

Cixous, Hélène. "Castration or Decapitation?" *Authorship: From Plato to the PostModern*. Ed. and Trans. Sean Burke. Edinburgh: Edinburgh University Press, 1995. 162-77.

___. *"Coming to Writing" and Other Essays*. Ed. Deborah Jenson. Trans. Sarah Cornell, Ann Liddle, and Susan Sellers. Cambridge: Harvard University Press, 1991.

___. *La* . Paris: des femmes, 1979.

___. "The Laugh of the Medusa." *Signs: Journal of Women in Culture and Society* 1 (Summer 1976): 875-93.

___. *The Newly Born Woman*. Trans. Betsy Wing. Minneapolis: Minnesota University Press, 1986.

Cunneen, Sally. *In Search of Mary: The Woman and the Symbol*. New York: Ballantine, 1996.

Danielson, Dennis, ed. *The Cambridge Companion to Milton*, 2nd ed. Cambridge: Cambridge University Press, 1999.

Danson, Lawrence. *Tragic Alphabet: Shakespeare's Drama of Language*. New Haven: Yale University Press, 1974.

Delaney, Sheila. *Impolitic Bodies: Poetry, Saints, and Society in Fifteenth-Century England.* New York: Oxford University Press, 1998.

Dolan, Frances E. "Women on Scaffolds." *Modern Philology* 92 (November 1994): 157-78.

Eilberg-Schwartz, Howard and Wendy Doniger. *Off with Her Head!: The Denial of Women's Identity in Myth, Religion and Culture.* Berkeley: University of California Press, 1995.

Ellinghausen, Laurie. "Literary Property and the Single Woman in Isabella Whitney's *A Sweet Nosegay.*" *SEL 1500-1900* 45.1 (Winter 2005): 1-22.

Ferguson, Margaret W. "The Spectre of Resistance." *Staging the Renaissance: Reinterpretations of Elizabethan and Jacobean Dramas.* Ed. David Scott Kastan and Peter Stallybrass. New York: Routledge, 1991. 235-50.

___ and Barry Weller, eds. *The Tragedy of Mariam, the Fair Queen of Jewry with The Lady Falkland; Her Life.* Berkeley: University of California Press, 1994.

Fischer, Sandra K. "Elizabeth Cary and Tyranny, Domestic and Religious." In *Silent But For The Word.* Ed. Margaret Hannay. Kent: Kent State University Press, 1985. 225-89.

Forget, Christopher Daniel Michael. *Adam and Eve: Ascending to the Godhead (An Analysis of the Fall in John Milton's Paradise Lost).* Huntington: Marshall University Press, 1994.

Foucault, Michel. *The Order of Things: An Archaeology of the Human Sciences.* New York: Random House, 1994.

Frye, Roland Mushat. *Milton's Imagery and the Visual Arts: Iconographic Tradition in the Epic Poems.* Princeton: Princeton University Press, 1978.

Furman, Wendy. "'Consider First, that Great/or Bright Infers not Excellence': Mapping the Feminine in Mary Groom's Miltonic Cosmos." *Milton Studies* 28 (1992): 21-62.

Gallagher, Philip J. *Milton, the Bible, and Misogyny.* Columbia: University of Missouri Press, 1990.

Gajowski, Evelyn. *The Art of Loving: Female Subjectivity and Male Discursive Traditions in Shakespeare's Tragedies.* Newark: University of Delaware Press, 1992.

___. "Lavinia as 'Blank Page': Voicelessness, Violation, and Violence in *Titus Andronicus.*" Paper delivered at the annual meeting of the Shakespeare Association of America, Montreal, April 2000. 1-21.

Gilbert, Sandra M. and Susan Gubar. *The Madwoman in the Attic.* New Haven: Yale University Press, 1979.

Gosenhill, Edward. *The Schoolhouse of Women.* London: W. Lynne, 1550.

Green, Douglas E. "Interpreting 'her martyr'd signs': Gender and Tragedy in *Titus Andronicus.*" *Shakespeare Quarterly* 40 (1989): 317-26.

Gubar, Susan. "'The Blank Page' and the Issues of Female Creativity." In *The New French Criticism: Essays on Women, Literature and Theory.* Ed. Elaine Showalter. New York: Pantheon Books, 1985. 292-313.

Hamington, Maurice. *Hail Mary? The Struggle for Ultimate Womanhood in Catholicism.* New York: Routledge, 1995.

Harrison, Barbara Grizzuti. "My Eve, My Mary." *Newsweek* (25 August 1997): 56.

Haslem, Lori Schroeder. "'Troubled with the Mother': Longings, Purgings, and the Maternal Body in *Bartholomew Fair* and *The Duchess of Malfi.*" *Modern Philology* 92 (May 1995): 438-57.

Heller, Jennifer Louise. "Space, Violence, and Bodies in Middleton and Cary." *SEL1500-1900* 45.2 (Spring 2005): 425-41.

Hibbard, George Richard, ed. *Three Renaissance Pamphlets.* New York: Books for Libraries Press, 1969.

Hinckeldey, Christoph. *Criminal Justice Through the Ages: From Divine Judgment to Modern German Legislation.* Federal Republic of Germany: Mittelalterliches Kriminalmuseum, 1981.

Hulse, S. Clark. "Wresting the Alphabet: Oratory and Action in *Titus Andronicus.*" *Criticism* 21 (1979): 106-18.

Hutcherson, Dudley R. "Milton's Eve and the Other Eves." *Studies in English, Mississippi University* 1 (1960): 12-31.

Hutson, Lorna. "Rethinking the 'Spectacle of the Scaffold': Juridical Epistemologies and English Revenge Tragedy." *Representations* 89 (Winter 2005): 30-58.

James, Heather. *Shakespeare's Troy: Drama, Politics and the Translation of Empire.* Cambridge: Cambridge University Press, 1997.

Jardine, Lisa. *Still Harping on Daughters: Women and Drama in the Age of Shakespeare.* New York: Columbia University Press, 1989.

Jolly, Penny Howell. *Made in God's Image? Eve and Adam in the Genesis Mosaics at San Marco, Venice.* Berkeley: University of California Press, 1997.

Jones, Ann Rosalind. "Apostrophes to Cities: Urban Rhetorics in Isabella Whitney and Moderata Fonte." *Attending to Early Modern Women.* Ed. Susan D. Amussen and Adele Seeff. London: Associated University Presses, 1998. 155-75.

___. "Writing to Live." In *The Currency of Eros: Women's Love Lyric in Europe 1540-1620.* Indianapolis: Indiana University Press, 1990. 36-52.

Josephus, Flavius. *The Antiquities of the Jews.* Ed. Samuel Burder. Boston: Joseph Teal, 1823.

Kahn, Coppelia. *Roman Shakespeare: Warriors, Wounds, and Women.* New York: Routledge 1997.

Kent, David A., ed. *The Achievement of Christina Rossetti.* Ithaca: Cornell University Press, 1987.

Kermode, Frank. "Toe-Lining." *London Review of Books* (22 January 1998): 9-10.

Kilgour, Maggie. "'Thy Perfect Image Viewing': Poetic Creation and Ovid's Narcissus in *Paradise Lost*." *Studies in Philology* 102.3 (Summer 2005): 307-39.

Kinney, Arthur F. *The Cambridge Companion to English Literature 1500-1600.* Cambridge: Cambridge University Press, 2000.

Kolodny, Annette. "Dancing Through the Minefield." *The New Feminist Criticism: Essays on Women, Literature and Theory.* Ed. Elaine Showalter. New York: Pantheon, 1985. 144-67.

Kothe, Ana. "Modest Incursion: The Production of Writers and their Readers in the Early Modern Prefaces of Isabella Whitney and Margaret Tyler." *English Language Notes* 37 (September 1999): 15-38.

Kristeva, Julia. *Powers of Horror: An Essay on Abjection.* Trans. by Leon S. Roudiez. New York: Columbia University Press, 1982.

Krontiris, Tina. *Oppositional Voices: Women as Writers and Translators of Literature in the English Renaissance.* London: Routledge, 1992.

Lamb, Mary Ellen. "The Countess of Pembroke and the Art of Dying." In *Gender and Authorship in the Sidney Circle.* Madison: University of Wisconsin Press, 1990. 207-26.

Lewalski, Barbara K. "Milton on Women - Yet Once More." *Milton Studies* VI (1975): 3-20.

Lincoln, Bruce. *Death, War, and Sacrifice: Studies in Ideology and Practice.* Chicago: University of Chicago Press, 1991.

Loughlin, Marie H. *Hymeneutics: Interpreting Virginity on the Early Modern Stage.* Lewisburg: Bucknell University Press, 1997.

MacKinnon, Catharine. "Feminism, Marxism, Method and the State." In *Feminism and Sexuality.* Ed. Stevi Jackson and Sue Scott. New York: Columbia University Press, 1996. 182-90.

McGrath, Lynnette F. "Isabella Whitney and the Ideologies of Writing and Publication." In *Teaching Tudor and Stuart Women.* Ed. Suzanne Woods and Margaret P. Hannay. New York: MLA, 2000. 283-8.

Male, Emile. *Religious Art from the Twelfth to the Eighteenth Century.* New York: The Noonday Press, 1949.

Marquis, Paul A. "Oppositional Ideologies of Gender in Isabella Whitney's *Copy of a Letter.*" *Modern Language Review* 90 (April 1995): 314-24.

Martin, Randall, ed. *Women Writers in Renaissance England*. New York: Addison Wesley Longman Limited, 1997.

Miller, Naomi J. "Domestic Politics in Elizabeth Cary's *The Tragedy of Mariam*." *Studies in English Literature 1500-1900* 37(1997): 353-69.

Milton, John. *The Complete Poetry of John Milton*. Ed. John T. Shawcross. Lexington: University Press of Kentucky, 1993.

Minh-ha, Trinh T. *Woman, Native, Other. Writing Postcoloniality and Feminism*. Bloomington: Indiana University Press, 1989.

Moi, Toril. *Sexual/Textual Politics: Feminist Literary Theory*. New York: Routledge, 2002.

Montaigne, Michel de. *An Apologie of Raymond Sebond*. Trans. Roger Ariew and Marjorie Grene. Indianapolis: Hackett Publishing Company Inc., 2003.

Murfin, Ross. "What is Psychoanalytic Criticism?" In *Hamlet: Case Studies in Contemporary Criticism* by William Shakespeare. Ed. Susanne L. Wofford. New York: St. Martin's Press, 1994. 241-51.

Ovid. *Ars Amatoria*. Trans. James Michie. New York: Modern Library, 2002.

___. *Metamorphoses*. Trans. Allen Mandelbaum. New York: Harcourt Brace, 1993.

Orlin, Lena Cowen. "Chronicles of Private Life." Kinney 241-64.

Patrides, C.A. *Milton and the Christian Tradition*. Oxford: Clarendon Press, 1966.

Patterson, Annabel, ed. *John Milton*. London: Longman Group UK Limited, 1992.

Pecheux, Sister Mary Christopher. "The Concept of the Second Eve in *Paradise Lost*." *PMLA* 75 (1960): 359-66.

Petit, Herbert H. "The Second Eve in *Paradise Regained*." *Papers of the Michigan Academy of Sciences, Arts and Letters* XLIV (1959): 365-69.

Phillippy, Patricia. "The Maid's Lawful Liberty: Service, the Household, and 'Mother B' in Isabella Whitney's *A Sweet Nosegay.*" *Modern Philology* 95 (May 1998): 439-62.

Radzinowicz, Mary Ann. "How Milton Read the Bible." Danielson (1999): 202-18.

Romeo, Caterina. "Engendering Silence, Articulating Alternative Languages: Lavinia in *Titus Andronicus*, Philomela in *The Metamorphoses*, and Marianna in *La Lunga Vita.*" *Exit 9, The Rutgers Journal of Comparative Literature* 6 (2004): 83-98.

Rowe, Katherine. *Dead Hands: Fictions of Agency, Renaissance to Modern.* Stanford: Stanford University Press, 1999.

Shakespeare, William. *The Riverside Shakespeare.* Ed. G. Blakemore Evans and J. J. M. Tobin. Boston: Houghton Mifflin Company, 1997.

Shawcross, John T. *John Milton: The Self and the World.* Lexington: University Press of Kentucky, 1993.

Showalter, Elaine. "Representing Ophelia: Women, Madness, and the Responsibilities of Feminist Criticism." Wofford 220-40.

Smith, Elise Lawton. "Women and the Moral Argument of Lucas Van Leyden's *Dance Around the Golden Calf.*" *Art History* 15 (Sept. 1992): 296-316.

Smith, J.C. and Carla J. Ferstman. *The Castration of Oedipus: Feminism, Psychoanalysis, and the Will to Power.* New York: New York University Press, 1996.

Starks, Lisa. "*Powers of Horror* and Horrors of Power in Julie Taymor's *Titus.*" Paper delivered at the annual meeting of the Shakespeare Association of America, Montreal, April 2000. 1-10.

Swaim, Kathleen M. "Flower, Fruit, and Seed: A Reading of *Paradise Lost.*" *Milton Studies* V (1973): 155-76.

Taymor, Julie, director. *Titus.* Anthony Hopkins, Jessica Lange, and Alan Cummings. Clear Blue Sky Productions, December 1999.

Tillyard, E. M. W. *The Elizabethan World Picture.* New York: Random House, 1942.

Travitsky, Betty, ed. *Paradise of Women: Writings by Englishwomen of the Renaissance*. Westport: Greenwood Press, 1981.

Tricomi, Albert H. "The Aesthetics of Mutilation in *Titus Andronicus*." *Shakespeare and Language* (2004): 226-39.

Valentis, Mary and Anne Devane. *Female Rage: Unlocking Its Secrets, Claiming its Power*. NY: Carol Southern Books, 1994.

Waddington, Raymond. "Rewriting the World, Rewriting the Body." Kinney 287-308.

Walker, Kim. *Women Writers of the English Renaissance*. New York: Twayne Publishers, 1996.

Wall, Wendy. "Authorship and the Material Conditions of Writing." Kinney 64-86.

Webber, Joan Mallory. "The Politics of Poetry: Feminism and *Paradise Lost*." *Milton Studies* (1980): 3-29.

Whitney, Isabella. Selected poems. *Women Writers in Renaissance England*. Ed. Randall Martin. New York: Addison Wesley Longman Limited, 1997.

Williamson, Beth. "Re: Virgin Mary as Eve." 1p. *Webcrawler*. Online. Internet.4Mar2000.<ukans.edu/~medieval/melcher/matthias/ı109/0 357.html>.

Wind, Edgar. *Pagan Mysteries in the Renaissance*. New Haven: Yale University Press, 1958.

Wittig, Monique. *Les Guerilleres*. Boston: Beacon, 1985.

Wittreich, Joseph Anthony. *Feminist Milton*. London: Cornell University Press, 1987.

Wofford, Susanne L., ed. *Case Studies in Contemporary Criticism: William Shakespeare* Hamlet. New York: St. Martin's Press, 1994.

Wollstonecraft, Mary. *A Vindication of the Rights of Women*. New York: Alfred A. Knopf, Inc., 1992.

Woolf, Virginia. *A Room of One's Own*. New York: Harcourt Inc., 1981.

Zimmerman, Shari A. "Disaffection, Dissimulation, and the Uncertain Ground of Silent Dismission: Juxtaposing John Milton and Elizabeth Cary." *ELH* 66.3 (Fall 1999): 553-89.

STUDIES IN ENGLISH LITERATURES

Edited by Koray Melikoğlu

ISSN 1614-4651

FORTHCOMING (MANUSCRIPT WORKING TITLES)

Paola Baseotto
Spenserian Views of Death
ISBN 3-89821-567-9

Kevin Cole
Levity's Rainbow
Menippean Poetics in Swift, Fielding, and Sterne
ISBN 3-89821-654-3

Series Subscription

Please enter my subscription to the series **Studies in English Literatures**, ISSN 1614-4651, as follows:

❏ complete series   OR   ❏ English-language titles

                                              ❏ German-language titles

starting with
❏ volume # 1
❏ volume # ___
     ❏ please also include the following volumes: #___, ___, ___, ___, ___, ___,
___

❏ the next volume being published
     ❏ please also include the following volumes: #___, ___, ___, ___, ___, ___,
___

❏ 1 copy per volume   OR   ❏ ___ copies per volume

Subscription within Germany:

You will receive every title on 1st publication at the regular bookseller's price incl. s & h and VAT.

Payment:
❏ Please bill me for every volume.
❏ Lastschriftverfahren; Ich/wir ermächtige(n) Sie hiermit widerruflich, den Rechnungsbetrag je Band von meinem/unserem folgendem Konto einzuziehen.

Kontoinhaber: _____ Kreditinstitut: _____
Kontonummer: _____ Bankleitzahl: _____

International Subscription:

Payment (incl. s & h and VAT) in advance for
❏ 10 volumes/copies (€ 319.80)   ❏ 20 volumes/copies (€ 599.80)
❏ 40 volumes/copies (€ 1,099.80)
Please send my books to:

NAME_____ DEPARTMENT_____
ADDRESS _____
POST/ZIP CODE_____ COUNTRY _____
TELEPHONE _____ EMAIL_____

date/signature_____

Please fax to: **0511 / 262 2201 (+49 511 262 2201)**
or mail to: *ibidem*-Verlag, Julius-Leber-Weg 11, D-30457 Hannover, Germany
or send an e-mail: ibidem@ibidem-verlag.de

***ibidem*-Verlag**

Melchiorstr. 15

D-70439 Stuttgart

info@ibidem-verlag.de

www.ibidem-verlag.de
www.edition-noema.de
www.autorenbetreuung.de